SIX ENERGY POLICIES TO SAVE THE PLANET

With a Foreword by Dr Fatih Birol

SIX ENERGY POLICIES TO SAVE THE PLANET

Neil A C Hirst
Imperial College London, UK

World Scientific

NEW JERSEY • LONDON • SINGAPORE • BEIJING • SHANGHAI • HONG KONG • TAIPEI • CHENNAI • TOKYO

Published by

World Scientific Publishing Europe Ltd.
57 Shelton Street, Covent Garden, London WC2H 9HE
Head office: 5 Toh Tuck Link, Singapore 596224
USA office: 27 Warren Street, Suite 401-402, Hackensack, NJ 07601

Library of Congress Cataloging-in-Publication Data
Names: Hirst, Neil, author.
Title: Six energy policies to save the planet / Neil A.C. Hirst, Imperial College London, UK ; with a foreword by Dr. Fatih Birol.
Description: New Jersey : World Scientific, [2024] | Includes bibliographical references and index.
Identifiers: LCCN 2024000585 | ISBN 9781800614994 (hardcover) | ISBN 9781800615038 (paperback) | ISBN 9781800615007 (ebook) | ISBN 9781800615014 (ebook other)
Subjects: LCSH: Energy policy--Environmental aspects. | Climatic changes--Environmental aspects.
Classification: LCC HD9502.A2 H543 2024 | DDC 333.79--dc23/eng/20240215
LC record available at https://lccn.loc.gov/2024000585

British Library Cataloguing-in-Publication Data
A catalogue record for this book is available from the British Library.

For any available supplementary material, please visit
https://www.worldscientific.com/worldscibooks/10.1142/Q0443#t=suppl

Desk Editors: Logeshwaran Arumugam/Rosie Williamson/Shi Ying Koe

Typeset by Stallion Press
Email: enquiries@stallionpress.com

Foreword

Neil Hirst's new book *Six Energy Policies to Save the Planet* provides a thoughtful and timely analysis of the issues facing energy policymakers today.

The world has made remarkable progress towards tackling climate change in recent years. The Paris Agreement has provided the accepted framework for governments to set national net zero emissions targets. Renewables have now, in many situations, become the lowest cost source of energy, and global clean energy investment now exceeds investment in fossil fuels. The remorseless growth of CO_2 emissions has slowed and may be about to stabilise, even as economic growth continues.

In other circumstances, all this would be a source of congratulation. But the task of transforming the global economy is so profound that it can only be regarded as the starting point. Much more is needed. To limit global warming to 1.5° or even 2.0°C, we now need to turn the corner and achieve an immediate and sharp decline in the rate of emissions.

The environment for energy policy-making is complex and demanding. Governments still have to provide the fundamentals of affordability, reliability, and energy security. But now they also have to achieve a rapid reduction in fossil fuel emissions. The policies must be fair and publicly acceptable, and they must be supportive of the global effort. It's a tough challenge.

This book analyses some of the most important policy areas. The first is to accelerate what we are doing already, especially in the adoption of renewables and the promotion of energy efficiency. The second is to invest boldly in the new technologies that are needed to complement renewables, notably hydrogen, carbon capture and storage, electricity storage, low-carbon fuels, and, where this is acceptable, nuclear power. The third is to persuade the public of the need for change. The transition offers major environmental and economic benefits. But governments and influencers have to recognise that it will require significant adaptation on the part of energy consumers. The fourth is strong economic and regulatory action to empower businesses to drive the transition. The precise mix has to be carefully judged in the light of national circumstances and traditions and what is most acceptable to the public. The fifth is for the developed nations to support the developing countries because climate policy only makes sense as a global effort. Opening the door for large-scale private sector investment should be the ultimate aim. The sixth and final policy is to strengthen international cooperation on the delivery of national targets.

The IEA is the leading international body supporting governments as they wrestle with these challenges. We are now entering a new phase in which we will evolve our mission and impact to further enhance this work. The increasing membership of our Association means that we are working, increasingly, with major developing as well as developed economies. This book has its own proposals for enhancing the role of the IEA.

Six Energy Policies to Save the Planet offers a deep insight into the complex and wide-ranging issues of energy policy that underly the global climate effort. I warmly recommend it to policymakers and influencers, as well as students and others with a serious interest in the climate challenge.

Dr Fatih Birol
Executive Director of the International Energy Agency

About the Author

Neil A C Hirst is an expert on international energy policy, originally working as a senior UK government official. He is a former Director for Technology and Global Dialogue at the International Energy Agency. He was the Energy Counsellor at the British Embassy in Washington and he was the Chairman of the G8 Nuclear Safety Working Group. He has worked on energy finance on secondment to Goldman Sachs in New York and as a contractor to the World Bank. Most recently he has been working with China's Energy Research Institute of the National Development and Reform Commission (NDRC) on a project funded by the UK's Foreign, Commonwealth and Development Office on China's role in global energy governance.

Neil Hirst has a first-class degree from Oxford in Politics, Philosophy, and Economics, and an MBA from Cornell USA. He is an Honorary Senior Research Fellow of Imperial College London. His previous book, *The Energy Conundrum: Climate Change, Global Prosperity, and the Tough Decisions We Have to Make*, was published by World Scientific in 2018. He is the joint author, with Prof. Yufeng Yang, of *Global Energy Governance Reform and China's Participation*, published by Tsinghua University Press in 2017.

Sources and Acknowledgements

Major sources are the IEA's two annual publications, World Energy Outlook (WEO) and Energy Technology Perspectives (ETP), the various report of the US Government's Energy Information Administration, BP's annual Energy Outlook and Statistical Review of World Energy, and the reports of the Intergovernmental Panel on Climate Change. I also recommend the annual Human Development Reports of the United Nations Development Programme (UNDP) and the World Bank's Human Development Reports. Our World in Data is an excellent source of data which also provided most of the charts.

Thanks are due to my wife Caroline for her patience during the long composition of this book and also for many valuable discussions of themes and messages. Also to friends and colleagues who have most kindly read manuscripts at various stages and offered comments and corrections, specifically my brother Ian, Graham White CBE, John and Sue Neve, and Tim Yarker. Thanks also to Rosie Williamson and Logesh Arumugam, Production Editors at World Scientific Publishing for much helpful guidance and for seeing the book through to its publication.

Contents

Introduction: The Six Policies

We are at the crossroads. 25 years since world leaders promised, in the UNFCCC[1] Climate Treaty, to stabilise greenhouse gas concentrations at safe levels, the rate of emissions has increased by 50% and it is still rising. "The spirit is willing but the flesh is weak".

This book is concerned with emissions arising from the production and use of energy, which account for at least two thirds of total greenhouse gas emissions. Emissions from farming, forestry, and land use are also important, but they are not the subject of this book. Similarly, the book does not cover adaptation to climate change, which has now become an equally urgent and important topic.

Energy from burning hydrocarbons, coal, oil, and gas, is a fundamental part of our way of life. It was the basis of the industrial revolution, which changed the world in ways that are both good and bad. It has raised living standards in the West to levels that were unimaginable in the pre-industrial era and to which developing nations now aspire. But it has caused severe environmental degradation and threatens the climate and the planet. Now we are facing the need, urgently, to do without these fuels.

The damage that has already been done cannot be reversed in our lifetimes. If our civilisation continues to flourish, future generations may view with dismay the failure of our generation to arrest global warming while the opportunity still existed. They may also be dismayed that we, in the developed world, tolerated the continuation of poverty for such a large part of the global population. These are not separate issues because in the developing world energy transition is about economic development first and climate mitigation second. As the Secretariat of the Climate Treaty has noted, transition will require "Integrated … solutions that promote the eradication of poverty, sustainable development for all, and the protection of natural resources and systems".[2]

Year after year the International Energy Agency (IEA) and other forecasters have called for urgent change and offered "sustainable" projections in which emissions go into immediate and sharp decline. And year after year emissions have continued to rise and the cliff down which they will need to fall gets steeper and steeper.

An urgent change of course is needed to save us from a global warming catastrophe. Governments are setting positive targets for the medium and longer term but so far their actions to meet these targets fall well short of what is needed. Until there is credible implementation the value of these targets remains questionable. We have to change course right now.

The Policies

Here are the six key policies needed to reverse the trend of growing emissions and save the planet;

(1) Accelerate
We are doing many of the right things. These include massive deployment of renewables, slowing and reversing the advance of coal, investing in energy efficiency. We are just not doing enough. We have to accelerate all these changes.

(2) Make Bold Investments in New Technologies
We still don't have all the technologies that we need. There are no proven solutions to the problems of renewable intermittency, of domestic and industrial heating, or, in part, of transport. Hydrogen, carbon sequestration, advanced nuclear, and perhaps other technologies waiting in the wings can provide the answers. Governments have to take the risk of investing in the massive scale needed to bring them into play, even though we can't be sure which ones will be winners.

(3) Persuade the Public to Adapt
The public will have to accept new technologies for domestic heating and transport and conserve and recycle materials. They will also have to pay, through taxation and utility bills, for the energy transition. Governments and environmental activists can be optimistic about the longer term but they must also be realistic about what is required in

the immediate future. They have to persuade and convince the public of the need to adapt.

(4) Take Firm Regulatory Action
Business will have to implement the change. The leadership of top executives will be important. But as Adam Smith famously said, "It is not through the benevolence of the butcher ... that we expect our dinner, but from [his] regard to [his] own interest". Governments must create the right framework for low-carbon investment to make business sense. They will need to take bold regulatory and economic measures and stick to them in the face of inertia and negative lobbying.

(5) Support the Developing World
Climate justice and common humanity require that rich countries support the developing world. There are also compelling pragmatic reasons for doing so. Most of today's emissions and all the expected growth in emissions, are now in the developing world. Unless developing countries follow a low-carbon pathway the net zero efforts of rich countries will be in vain. This involves climate and development aid, and institutional support. It involves opening the door for private sector finance. We will need "innovative forms of ... cooperation" as the UNFCCC Secretariat have put it.[3]

(6) Raise the level of global cooperation
Climate mitigation is one of the greatest of human projects requiring profound changes to the global economy. International cooperation is essential. This especially includes cooperation between the West and China and cooperation between the developed and the developing countries. We have valued international institutions working in this field but they are not yet providing the sustained strategic coordination that is required. We need to strengthen the institutions of global energy governance.

These six actions are closely connected. Governments cannot stick to bold regulations without public support and technologies must be available to enable those affected to comply at acceptable cost. Without the technologies to manage intermittency, investment in variable renewables will inevitably wither. The public will not support tough domestic measures unless they see other countries making their contribution. As the impact of transition on national economies and trade becomes increasingly profound, so the need for international coordination will intensify.

The three fundamentals of energy policy — security of supply, environmental protection, and affordability — have not changed. They are not necessarily in conflict, but they have to be balanced. Security of supply has to be maintained because our economies and our way of life depend on it. Climate change has made environmental protection a top priority. Environmental measures can reinforce security. For instance, electric vehicles will not depend on imported oil, though they will need imported materials for their construction. Renewable electricity replaces gas but exposes us to the risks of variability. Affordability is a social and commercial necessity. Renewables hold out the prospect of affordable energy for the future but the low-carbon transition will be costly, and governments have to consider who should pay.

Current Pressures

Fossil fuels permeate almost all aspects of our modern economy. The transition to net zero, a state in which any continuing CO_2 emissions are matched by extraction of CO_2 from the atmosphere, requires profound political, economic, technical, social, and behavioural changes on a global scale. It's a tough call in a world that is riven with conflict and inequality and lacks strong international coordination. Other significant events affecting the global economy inevitably have their impact on the climate effort.

The COVID-19 epidemic was a vast human tragedy in which half a billion people were infected and six million people died.[4] For the first time in decades the steady improvement in the human condition and the reduction of world poverty were put into reverse. As a result of measures adopted in response to the epidemic, there was a sharp reduction in global emissions, but this proved to be short lived and by the end of 2021 emissions were exceeding pre-Covid levels. The rebound of coal consumption in China and India was particularly sharp.[5]

COVID-19 support measures have drained national resources that might have been available for energy transition. On the other hand governments in Europe the US and elsewhere have vowed to "build back better" with national recovery programmes that include green investment. If these programmes are successful, the COVID-19 epidemic, for all the tragedy involved,[6] may eventually have positive consequences for the climate.

Russia's 2022 invasion of Ukraine shattered energy markets and, for a time, re-directed government energy policies in a dash for short term security of supply. As the world's largest gas exporter and third largest oil exporter, after Saudi Arabia and the US, Russia is certainly a super-power in energy. High oil and gas prices and the fear of shortages have had both positive and negative effects on the climate effort. Looking to the future, the case for switching to renewables has been underlined, but in the short term governments are scrambling for supplies of whatever energy is available, including coal, oil, and gas. The UK, for instance, is postponing the closure of its remaining coal fired power stations and Germany is reopening mothballed coal plants. On the stock market, the assumption that green investments will automatically be more profitable than the oil gas and coal industries took a knock, as the profits of fossil energy companies swelled. That may not last.

The pandemic, and even more so the war in Ukraine, severely damaged international relationships. They increased the tensions between the West and the developing world — particularly China, India, and the Middle East — and this will only make collaboration on climate change more difficult. But these may be short term effects. If governments are prepared to plan for the longer term there can also be benefits.

Governments have also sought to maintain affordability through fossil fuel subsidies on a much larger scale than seen before. This should be a short term measure for use only in extreme circumstances. Until the crisis struck, the G20 had been campaigning against subsidies for fossil fuels. But it emphasises the importance of affordability and the role that governments need to play in determining how the carbon transition is to be financed.

A Global Problem

The climate problem also looks very different in different parts of the world. This is not just because of differing stages of economic development. Hot countries have different energy needs from cold countries. Some countries have mountainous regions that are suitable for hydro-electric power. Some are better endowed than others with coal, oil, or gas. Wind and solar conditions also vary and some countries have suitable coasts for offshore installations. Some countries are also more vulnerable to climate change than others. Political factors also come into play. Nuclear power is not an acceptable option in some countries. This book is global in scope, but it also focuses on the situation in different countries and regions.

Developed economies, including the UK, will have to give a lead. They created the problem and they have the technical, financial and administrative capability to transform the way energy is produced and used. Otherwise we cannot expect other nations still going through their industrial revolutions, and with far fewer resources, to take up the challenge.

Profound global change is imperative in the light of what we now know about the causes and consequences of global warming. It cannot be achieved without international cooperation, which requires a degree of mutual understanding and good will. If we do succeed, the benefits will be far reaching. Besides protecting the climate, we can improve local environments and generate new business and personal opportunities. Success in addressing climate change can also contribute to progress on some of the world's other most intractable problems, notably the mistrust between developed and developing nations and between China and the West, and the severe inequality of living standards. It isn't a panacea, but it can contribute. The world can be a nicer place. On the other hand failure to control climate change, with its severe consequences especially in less developed regions, is bound to exacerbate international tension.

The global response to the climate challenge, and the achievements of climate diplomacy, have been truly remarkable. We should not lose sight of that. In other circumstances they would be a cause for celebration. But the task of transforming the global energy economy is so vast that efforts still fall far short of what is required.

In the last year or two we have seen increasingly grave manifestations of climate change. There has been a significant change in the public mood and a growing recognition of the urgency of the threat. Hopefully we are turning a corner. It seems unlikely that we will succeed in containing global warming to 1.5°, the target set by world governments. This is a reason to redouble our efforts to avoid even greater disaster. But we must also consider the implications of not reaching these targets. For some countries the consequences would be extreme. Countries with the technological means to do so might decide to embark on unilateral action through geoengineering, in other words direct interference with the atmosphere. Such a step would be fraught with danger. It is not too soon to start considering now the global governance for controlling such measures.

We have almost certainly left it too late. There will be severe consequences. But international efforts may succeed in limiting global warming to well below the truly catastrophic levels that we are heading for today. That is what we are fighting for now.

Chapter 1

Where Are We Now? Big Achievements But Still Not Nearly Enough

Key Policy No. 1.

We are doing many of the right things. The framework for climate diplomacy is in place. We have made spectacular progress in commercialising renewables and reducing their costs. Governments have policies for improving energy efficiency. But so far these efforts are far from matching the challenge. Trends in CO_2 emissions are still largely driven by demography and economic development rather than climate mitigation efforts. The increase in the rate of emissions has slowed but we have still not turned the corner for the sharp downward shift that is needed for net zero. We are doing the right things but not yet on the necessary scale, and we are far from being on track to net zero.

Introduction

We have made a lot of progress. National and international efforts have been impressive, and almost every nation now backs the framework set by the 2015 Paris Agreement under the Climate Treaty. The cost of renewables has fallen sharply with mass deployment. In 2021, about 80% of all investment in the world power system was in renewables, electric grids or storage.

But our efforts still do not come even close to measuring up to the scale of the challenge. According to the International Renewable Energy Agency (IRENA), we would need to triple the rate at which we are adding renewable generating capacity to be on course for the 1.5°C target.

Renewable electricity is the brightest spot in our climate efforts. We have made much less progress in other major areas, such as transport, industry, heating, and cooling. Another major indicator of progress, the rate of improvement of energy efficiency, has actually declined to an average of 1% p.a. since 2017, compared to at least 3% p.a. that the IEA judged would be needed to meet governments' stated objectives.[7] Most of the changes in global emissions intensity thus far have been due to the natural evolution of economies as they develop rather than specific climate efforts. We are going to have to raise our game and do a lot more of the things that we are already doing.

Following the 2021 Glasgow Summit, governments set targets for the future that would be consistent with limiting global warming to 2°C, but the policies for meeting even this level of ambition are still in question.

World leaders are much better at setting long-term targets than they are at containing emissions today. As the rate of emissions and their impact on the climate continue to rise, the leaders have tightened the target from containing global warming to "well below 2°C" to 1.5°C. The divergence between aspiration and performance is increasing. "Between the idea and the reality … falls the shadow".[8] At some point, the experts will have to say, "You have left it too late". We are perilously close to that.

The mood in business, government, finance, and among the public is positive. Climate change is real; the danger is acute; strong action is required. Virtually every nation on earth is committed to climate mitigation in principle, even if one has to question whether this has yet flowed through to effective action. Leaders in business and government increasingly accept that the future is green and that those who do not adapt will be left behind. There is a scramble for leadership in the low-carbon technologies that are now being recognised as vital for economic progress. For almost all major nations, climate change has risen high on the agenda of geopolitics and national security.

The Climate Threat

In a previous book on energy policy,[9] I included a section explaining the nature of the climate threat. Now, this is hardly necessary. There is legitimate debate on the precise consequences of climate change, and most projections offer a range of outcomes. But nobody of goodwill and with even a modicum of access to scientific information can doubt the severity of the threat that we face or that it has been caused by human intervention.

The Intergovernmental Panel on Climate Change (IPCC) is a group of leading climate scientists from all over the world established by the UN and the World Meteorological Organization (WMO) to advise on climate change. As such, it represents mainstream expert climate opinion. It says that "global warming reaching 1.5° in the near term would cause unavoidable increases in multiple climate hazards. Beyond 2040, and depending on the level of global warming, climate change will lead to numerous risks to natural and human systems". These include lack of water, flood damage, food insecurity, especially in vulnerable regions, life-threatening heatwaves, threats to small islands and low-lying coasts from rising sea levels, and consequent displacement of people and involuntary migration.[10]

Africa is probably the most vulnerable continent. The IPCC report highlights three main threats. These are biodiversity loss and ecosystem disruption; mortality and morbidity from heat and infectious diseases; and reduced food production from crops and fisheries. These are judged "moderate" at the 1°C temperature increase that has already taken place, but "high" at 2°C. Even below that level, "the annual number of days above potentially lethal heat thresholds reaches 50–150 at 1.6°C in West Africa".

Europe is somewhat less vulnerable. "Southern regions tend to be more negatively affected while some benefits have been observed alongside negative impacts in northern and central regions". The main risks are as follows: mortality of people; disruption of ecosystems due to heat; loss of agricultural production due to heat and droughts; water scarcity; and floods. Damage from river and coastal flooding is projected to increase 20 times at 1.5–2.1°C and by "two or three orders of magnitude" at 2–3°C. However, the consequences of flooding can be substantially reduced by major investment in protection. The benefits, mainly in northern and central areas, include more comfortable temperatures (especially in the Autumn and Spring) less need for heating, and increased crop yields and forest growth due to the higher level of CO_2 in the atmosphere. The IPCC is clear that even in Europe the negative effects greatly outweigh the positive ones.

Taken as a whole, these are grave, indeed catastrophic threats. But does climate change represent an "existential threat" to mankind as world leaders such as Joe Biden[11] and UN Secretary-General Antonio Guterres[12] have said, and as the name of the environmental movement 'Extinction Rebellion' implies? That depends partly on how one interprets the phrase. If it means that the way of life and even the survival of large numbers of people are threatened, then yes, we face an existential threat. If it means an end to human life on earth, then the position is not so clear. The IPCC doesn't say that. However, there are reputable scientists who think that human life itself may be threatened because self-reinforcing feedback, in which the oceans and the land give up vast quantities of stored CO_2 and methane could lead to tipping points that "push the climate beyond human ability to control".[13]

The full consequences of failing to control global warming are hard to predict. We are entering uncharted territory. The well-established consequences are catastrophic enough.

These effects are already evident. According to the latest report of the IPCC,[14] "Widespread and rapid changes in the atmosphere, ocean, cryosphere and biosphere have occurred. Human-caused climate change is already affecting many weather and climate extremes in every region across the globe. This has led to widespread adverse impacts and related losses and damages to nature and people. Vulnerable communities who have historically contributed the least to current climate change are disproportionately affected". The changes include heatwaves, heavy precipitation, droughts, and tropical cyclones.

According to the *Lancet*,[15] "During 2021 and 2022, extreme weather events caused devastation across every continent, adding further pressure to health services already grappling with the impacts of the COVID-19 pandemic. Floods in Australia, Brazil, China, western Europe, Malaysia, Pakistan, South Africa, and South Sudan caused thousands of deaths, displaced hundreds of thousands of people, and caused billions of dollars in economic losses. Wildfires caused devastation in Canada, the USA, Greece, Algeria, Italy, Spain, and Türkiye, and record temperatures were recorded in many countries, including Australia, Canada, India, Italy, Oman, Türkiye, Pakistan, and the UK. With advancements in the science of detection and attribution studies, the influence of climate change over many events has now been quantified". The summer of 2023 again witnessed life-threatening high temperatures in Southern Europe, North Africa, and part of North America and Asia.

According to the IPCC,[16] human activities have already caused 1.0°C of global warming above pre-industrial levels and these effects will persist for "centuries to millennia".

Emission Trends

In the lead-up to the 2021 Glasgow Climate Summit, almost all major economies committed to achieving net-zero emissions during 2050–2070, with many regional and local governments and leading businesses in support. Commitments to reduce methane emissions and coal consumption were useful even though some of the main emitters did not sign up for them. India made an important announcement on solar energy. According to the IEA, if all the targets that governments have now announced were met, global warming would be contained to below 2°C. Without doubt, that would be a truly massive achievement.

Yet, the situation today is disappointing. More than 25 years after the Climate Treaty was signed, global emissions are still rising. The developed nations have failed to come up with the $100 billion p.a. promised at the Copenhagen Climate Summit in 2009 to support poorer nations. This is most disappointing, particularly given the climate rhetoric that has been adopted by countries such as the US, Japan, Germany, France, and the UK, all of which have multi-trillion dollar economies.

The central aim of the Glasgow Summit was for nations to "ratchet up" their targets for emissions reduction by 2030, which many states have done. However, it was a disappointment that China, the largest emitter, did not bring forward its target that emissions will peak by 2030 and that Xi Jinping did not attend in person. The IEA's analysis of energy policies in place today, as distinct from long-term targets, shows global warming continuing its rise to well over 2°.

"Blah, Blah, Blah", says Greta Thunberg.[17] That isn't a fair summary and, I suppose, it's not intended to be. However, the targets have been pushed into the future and it is far from clear how they are going to be met. It would be wrong to underestimate the progress that has been made so far even while we recognise that it is not nearly enough. "Give me chastity, Oh Lord, but not yet", prayed St Augustine.

The Climate Treaty[18] was signed in 1992. Its overall objective was to "stabilise greenhouse gas concentrations in the atmosphere at levels that will prevent dangerous anthropomorphic interference with the climate system". More than 30 years later, how successful has it been?

Since the Treaty was agreed, the World's annual emissions of CO_2 from fossil fuels have risen from 23 billion tonnes p.a. to 36 billion tonnes p.a., an increase of more than 50%.[19] The average increase in CO_2 concentrations in the atmosphere has steadily accelerated from 1.5% p.a. between 1990 and 2000 to 2.4% between 2010 and 2020.[20] The effects of human-caused global warming are happening now, are irreversible on the timescale of people alive today, and will worsen in the decades to come.[21] You can argue that the Treaty has already failed in its mission.

This is a reason to redouble our efforts and not to ease off. The house is already on fire. The inhabitants are at risk. We have to act with urgency.

Why have emissions continued to rise in this remorseless way despite the good intentions of almost every nation on earth?

Historically, the big drivers of CO_2 emissions in the World have been the increase in population and rising prosperity, measured as GDP per person. Declining energy intensity, or energy per unit of GDP, has been insufficient to counteract these effects. Thus, between 2000 and 2019, the world population rose by 25%, and GDP per person increased by 45%. Between 1980 and 2019, the proportion of people living in extreme poverty declined from over 40% to less than 9%. This was a big success for the human condition that is not as widely recognised as it should be. But it increased the climate threat because most of the gains were in coal-powered countries, such as China and India.

The first stages of economic development are energy-intensive. The construction of basic physical infrastructure – roads, railways, housing, electric power stations, industry, water, schools, and institutions of all kinds – requires large amounts of energy. As economies mature, they tend to become less energy-intensive. Relatively speaking, more money is spent on services and high value-added products and less on heavy industry, construction, and basic manufacturing, which are the biggest emitters. Thus, the energy intensity of global GDP fell by a quarter between 1980 and 2019. This was by far the biggest factor mitigating the rise in CO_2 emissions.[22] Nevertheless, emissions rose by 44% between 2000 and 2019.

Chart I shows the rapid rise in world energy consumption since 2065. Although consumption in Europe and the US has stabilised, global consumption has continued to increase rapidly, driven by the industrialisation of developing countries, of which China is the prime example.

Chart I.

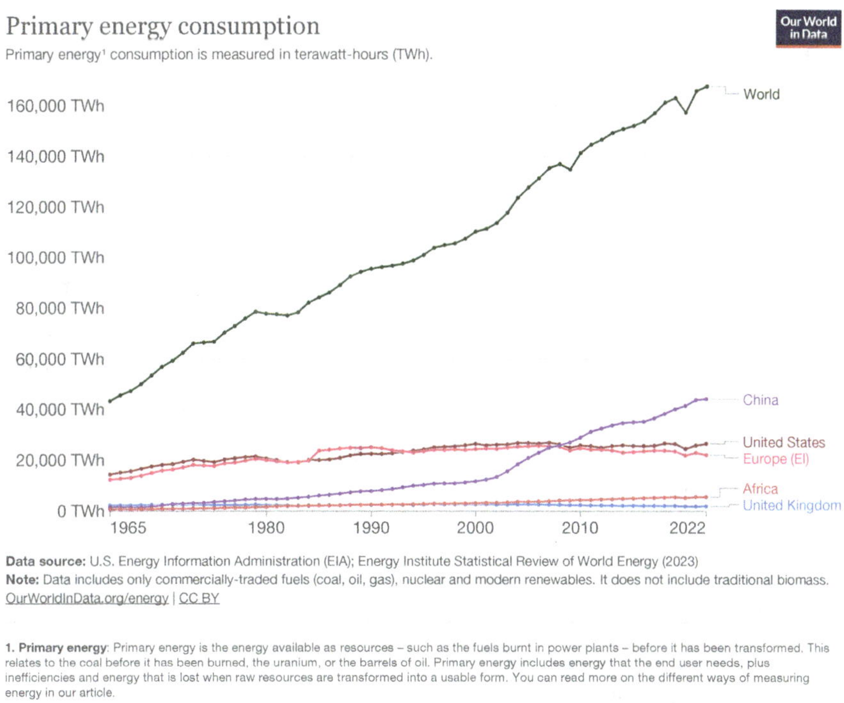

Chart II shows the rapid rise in global CO_2 emissions since about 1750. The trends largely reflect those of energy consumption, with Chinese emissions rising rapidly, while emissions from the US and Europe have begun to decline.

Chart II.

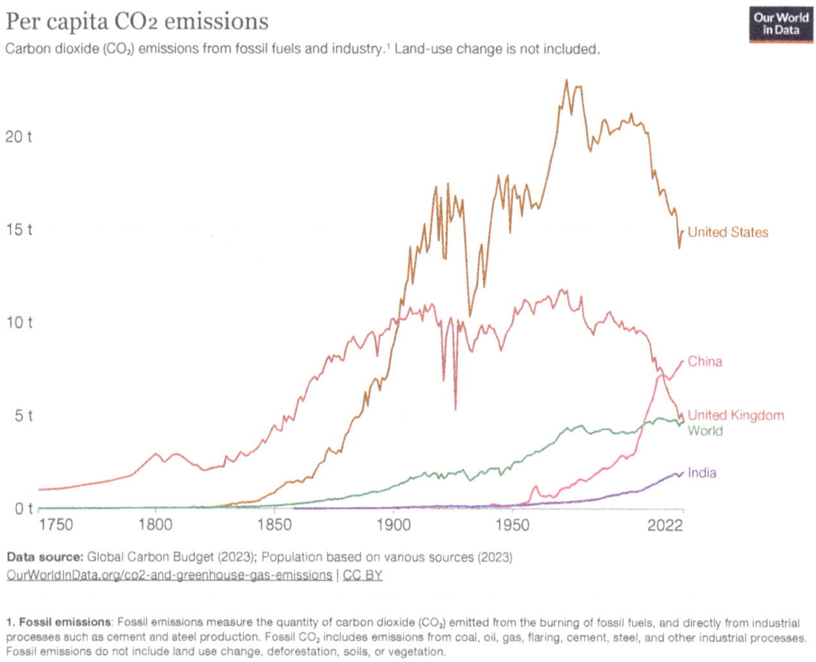

The consequence of these fundamental trends is that we have to run fast even to stand still on CO_2 emissions. We have to find low-carbon alternatives and efficiency gains to replace existing fossil fuel consumption. But we also have to deploy these alternatives fast enough to meet the rapid growth in energy demand as low- and medium-income economies in Asia, Africa, and South America pursue their ambitions for rapid economic growth.

The share of fossil fuels in world energy has been remarkably stable. As total world energy increased nearly three-fold between 1971 and 2022, the share of fossil fuels only declined from 87% to 80%. Renewables other than hydro- and biofuels, including wind and solar electricity, contributed only 2% of world energy in 2022, though of course, they were rising rapidly.[23] A fairer estimate of their contribution is that they contributed 11% to the world electricity supply in 2022, although this was still less than a third of the contribution of coal and less than half that of gas.

In general, changes in the carbon intensity of energy contributed much less to containing the growth of carbon emissions than changes in the energy intensity of GDP. In the US, the substitution of gas for coal has contributed significantly to reducing emissions from electricity generation. But generally, savings from using less energy per GDP were more significant than savings from switching to low-carbon sources. These savings arise partly from changes in the balances of economies, as described above, and partly from meeting the same energy needs more efficiently. This underlines the crucial role that energy efficiency has to play in reducing emissions.

Overall, in recent decades, emissions from the developed countries that belong to the Organisation for Economic Co-operation and Development (OECD) have gradually declined, reflecting the maturity of their economies, while those of developing non-OECD countries have increased. In 2005, the OECD countries emitted 13.4 Gigatonnes (Gt) of CO_2 from fuel combustion, but this had declined to 12.2 Gt in 2015. The non-OECD countries emitted 13.6 GT in 2005 rising to 20.1 Gt in 2015.

These figures do not take account of the fact that a significant share of emissions in non-OECD countries resulted from the production of goods to be exported and consumed in the OECD. If one attributes emissions to where goods are consumed, the OECD's emissions are increased by 1.6 Gt in 2005 and by 2.2 Gt in 2015 and the non-OECD's emissions are reduced by the same amounts. It's a significant difference, but it does not alter the overall trend that OECD emissions have been falling while non-OECD emissions are rising.[24]

The biggest increases have been seen in China and to a lesser extent India. While the US has achieved a significant reduction in its emissions since 1990 and in Europe emissions have almost halved, emissions from China have risen by about five times and emissions from India by about four times. This reflects the spectacular economic growth that these two countries have achieved, largely powered by coal which is abundant in both countries. Coal is the most polluting of the fossil fuels, and China alone now accounts for more than half of world coal consumption.

Before we are too censorious, we should recognise that the development of these two countries has lifted hundreds of millions of people, perhaps more than a billion, out of extreme poverty. The UN has described it as the greatest relief of poverty in world history. We should also remember that emissions per head in China today are well below those of the US and about on par with those of Europe. Emissions per head in India are a fraction of those in the developed world.

Measured in terms of emissions intensity, China's record is impressive. Emissions per unit of GDP more than halved between 2005 and 2020. That was not, mainly, the result of switching to low-carbon energy sources such as renewables. The main reason was a big reduction in China's energy intensity. In other words, China has greatly reduced the amount of energy required to produce one unit of GDP. Its economy has started to mature. The government has also undertaken a massive energy efficiency drive, of which the "Top 10,000 Energy Consuming Enterprises Programme" is the flagship. It is mainly these factors that have enabled the growth of China's emissions to begin levelling off – probably the most encouraging development in the global emissions scene – while economic growth has continued albeit at a reduced rate. They have also enabled China to more than achieve its target of reducing the carbon intensity of its economy by 45% from 2005 to 2020.

China is a massive player in the climate challenge, as will be illustrated repeatedly in this book. One can dwell on China's continuing high dependence on coal or on the great strides that China has made in deploying renewables and improving energy efficiency. The reality is that China is in the same position as most other major economies. China has made impressive progress, but it is still not nearly sufficient.

In the US, emissions per unit of GDP have approximately halved between 2000 and 2020, mostly due to a decrease in energy intensity but partly as a result of a decline in the carbon intensity of energy as coal has been displaced by gas and, to a lesser extent, renewables. There are legitimate concerns about the American shale gas revolution, especially the leakage of "fugitive" methane into the atmosphere, but so far, on balance, the American shale gas revolution has been good for the climate. Total CO_2 emissions in the US fell from 5.4 Gt in 2010 to 4.8 Gt in 2020. The biggest drivers in the US have been the competitiveness of its industries and the switch from coal to gas.

In India, carbon emissions from energy increased by 50% between 2000 and 2020 (from 1.7 Gt to 2.5 Gt) as a result of rapid economic growth and heavy reliance on coal. Although there was some decline in energy intensity, this was partly counteracted by an increase in the carbon intensity of energy as coal's share increased. The growth of solar power, discussed in detail later, is starting to have an impact. Due to their immense populations and relatively early-stage economies, India and Africa are now the regions with the greatest potential for increased carbon emissions if their governments do not pursue low-carbon energy policies.

Germany achieved a 15% reduction in emissions between 2010 and 2020, mainly due to a reduction in energy intensity (80% of the reduction) but to a more limited degree by switching to lower carbon technologies such as renewables (16% of the reduction). But Germany still has much higher emissions per person than other advanced European economies, such as the UK or France, because more than a quarter of Germany's electricity still comes from coal.

The UK achieved a 27% reduction in emissions from energy between 2010 and 2020, based, in part, on the virtual elimination of coal from power generation. However, reduced energy intensity still played a larger part in the UK's reduction in the carbon intensity of GDP, at 69%, compared to 30% for the reduced carbon intensity of energy. The EU as a whole achieved a 15% reduction in CO_2 emissions from 2010 to 2019.

For at least a decade, the IEA has been calling for urgent emissions reductions to meet the climate crisis. Each year it publishes a "sustainable" scenario showing what is needed. And each year emissions continue their remorseless rise. It's "a triumph of hope over experience", to use a well-known phrase.[25]

To get to really low levels of carbon emissions, we will need to accelerate the switch to renewables and other forms of low-carbon energy. In the rich developed world, we have to move rapidly to net zero. In the developing world, new low-carbon energy has to sustain rapid economic progress and poverty reduction as well as replace existing fossil fuel-based energy infrastructure. In other words, the carbon intensity of energy will have to change drastically. It's a big challenge.

Hitherto economic development has required a rapid growth in energy supply and a similarly rapid growth in carbon emissions. Today's developing economies are being asked to find a different path.

Here, we have a critical dilemma of climate policy: how to resolve the tension between prosperity and emissions reduction. That will be a constant theme of this book. Some will say that there is no such tension today because low-carbon options, such as wind and solar, are now fully competitive with fossil fuels, but it does not always appear so in the developing world. In countries with well-established domestic fossil fuel industries and those lacking the sophisticated grids that are needed to make the most of intermittent renewable energy, it is not so obvious that the low-carbon route is the most attractive. The fossil fuel industries are home-grown and come with existing employment and lobbying power, whereas renewables, at least initially, have to be imported and require foreign currency. Even in developed economies, we see that politicians, notwithstanding their green rhetoric, are not willing to adopt measures that might impact on energy security, jobs, or living standards.

Different countries have faced different challenges. Most West European countries had already run down their coal industries, for economic reasons, well before the climate crisis. Their heavily depleted deep mines could not compete with surface mines in Australia or Colombia as the economics of bulk coal shipment improved. It was, nevertheless, a painful process. In the UK, the closure of coal mines led to mass and sometimes violent demonstrations and created a deep sense of grievance in mining communities that persists to this day.

Germany is an exception, partly because of the integration of East Germany. Germany still generates over 30% of its electricity from lignite, which is the most polluting and carbon-emitting form of coal. One of the richest and most prosperous countries in the world is struggling to bring forward the final closure of its coal industry from 2038 to 2030.

While Western Europe and the US have made good progress in reducing coal demand, there has been no significant reduction in oil demand, mainly for transport and chemicals, over the past decade and gas demand in the US has risen rapidly as a result of the availability of cheap shale gas. In contrast, coal demand in China, India, and South East Asia has been rising rapidly over the past decade. In Europe and the US, oil is the largest source of CO_2 emissions, but in the world as a whole, it is coal. One of the more encouraging developments is that the growth in demand for coal in China seems to have been tailing off in the last few years. The rise of wind and solar power has been rapid right across the globe.

Different countries have, understandably, done what is easiest for them. In the West, the displacement of coal in power generation by gas and renewables has been economically attractive and, therefore, relatively painless, except for coal mining communities themselves. After the change in energy intensity, this has been the major source of emissions reductions in the world. In China and India, the situation has been quite different. Gas supplies have been limited, and although renewables have been making an increasing contribution to electricity supply, the rapid growth in electricity demand has meant that the demand for coal has not fallen. The most positive thing that one can say is that at least the growth of demand for coal in these countries, which has been driving the growth of world emissions in the last few decades, has slowed and consumption may be about to peak.

In sectors other than electricity generation, the performance of emissions reductions across the world has been poor. Europe has not so far made much progress in reducing emissions from industry, and no progress at all in reducing emissions from transport. The US has made some progress in reducing industrial emissions as natural gas has displaced coal and to some extent oil, but emissions from transport have continued to rise. Electric vehicles may hold out great promise for emissions reductions in the future, but, in the meanwhile, nobody has been brave enough to stem the rising tide of sports utility vehicles (SUVs), which accounted for a record 44% of new car sales in Europe in 2021. Light trucks (including crossovers and SUVs) accounted for 75% of US car sales in 2020.[26] In the US, transport is the biggest source of CO_2 emissions. In Europe, it is the second biggest after power.

So far, the switch to low-carbon energy sources, such as renewables, has played only a limited role in containing the growth of emissions, barely sufficient to keep up with the increase in energy demand. That will need to change. But even as we press forward with the adoption of low-carbon technologies, we should remember the importance of accelerating the existing trend of declining energy intensity. This includes not only conventional energy efficiency measures but also measures that are now attracting increasing interest such as recycling and reducing the energy needed for manufacturing, construction and packaging. In the short term, it is these measures that will probably yield the largest reductions in emissions. In the medium and longer term, reducing the carbon intensity of energy through the wholesale displacement of fossil energy with low-carbon alternatives will have to accelerate as we move to net zero.

Emissions may be on the decline in the US and Europe, and they may be peaking in China, but there is immense potential for emissions growth in populous parts of the world that are at an earlier stage of economic development, such as India, Africa, and parts of Asia. Achieving prosperity without rapid emissions growth in these regions is the next big challenge. It will be essential to improve energy efficiency, but low-carbon energy technologies will have to play a much bigger role than they have done so far. We are effectively asking these regions to "leap-frog" the carbon-based industrialisation that all developed nations have undergone. The developed countries will have to help with finance, technology, and administrative support. A step change is needed in the level of support, but the developed countries will be in no position to influence the development mode of emerging economies unless they first put their own houses in order and drastically reduce their own emissions.

Climate Negotiations

Figure 1 shows some of the main milestones in climate negotiations since the institution of the Intergovernmental Panel on Climate Change in 1988.

Figure 1. Climate Mitigation Timeline

1988
- Intergovernmental Panel on Climate Change (IPCC) established by the World Meteorological Organization and the UN

1990
- IPCC's First Report
  - Emissions from human activities "will result in additional warming of the Earth's surface".

1992
- United Nations Framework Convention on Climate Change is agreed at the UN Earth Summit
  - Objective is "stabilisation of the greenhouse gas concentrations in the atmosphere at a level that would prevent dangerous interference with the climate".
  - "Common but differentiated responsibilities". Developed countries must "take the lead" and provide "additional financial resources" to developing countries.
  - Measures must not constitute a "disguised restriction on international trade".

1997
- Kyoto Protocol to the UNFCCC adopted: the Protocol came into effect in 2005 when 55 countries signed
  - Participating developed countries, not including the US or China, accepted emissions limits. Trading mechanisms.
  - Emissions trading mechanisms adopted.
  - Two "commitment periods" from 2008 to 2012 and from 2012 to 2020.
  - Participation dwindled. The Protocol was overtaken by the Paris Agreement (see below) in 2015.

2009
- Copenhagen Conference of the Parties (COP) to the UNFCCC
  - Target of keeping global warming to "below 2°C".
  - Developed countries "Commit to a goal of mobilising jointly $100 billion p.a. by 2020 to address the needs of developing countries".

2011
- Durban COP
  - Commitment to make a new climate change agreement "with legal force", "applicable to all parties" to be agreed in 2015 and come into force by 2020.

2015
- UN unanimously adopts 17 Sustainable Development Goals (SDGs) including:
  - SDG No. 7 "Affordable and Clean Energy"
  - SDG No. 13 "Climate Action"
- Paris Agreement made at Paris COP
  - Target of containing global warming to "well below 2°C" with "efforts to limit to 1.5°C".
  - All parties, developed and developing, to submit climate plans, "Nationally Determined Contributions (NDCs)".
  - NDCs to be ratcheted up every five years.

2018
- IPCC Special Report on Global Warming of 1.5°C
  - "Robust differences" between the consequences of 1.5°C and 2.0°C global warming.

2021
- Glasgow COP (delayed from 2020 because of COVID-19)
  - Ratcheting up of NDCs plus most major countries announce longer-term targets to achieve net zero by 2050 or later.
  - IEA says that the new targets, if fully met on time would be sufficient to hold global warming below 2°C. "What is essential is that governments turn their pledges into clear and credible policy actions".
  - Refinement of Paris proposals for carbon trading.

2022
- IPCC Report on Mitigation
  - "Without immediate deep emissions reduction … limiting global warming to 1.5°C is beyond reach".
  - Global temperatures will stabilise when carbon dioxide emissions reach net zero. For 1.5°C this is needed by "the early 2050s", for 2.0°C "in the early 2070s".
- Sharm El-Sheikh COP
  - Developed countries agree in principle to set up a fund for the "loss and damage" suffered by developing nations from climate change.

The Climate Treaty, formally the United Nations Framework Convention on Climate Change, negotiated in 1992 and coming into force in 1994, was a remarkable achievement of international diplomacy. It brought virtually every nation on earth together with the agreed aim of achieving "stabilization of greenhouse gas concentrations in the atmosphere at a level that would prevent dangerous anthropomorphic interference with the climate system".

Inevitably, it had limitations and inherent tensions. The Treaty is a "framework" because it does not contain any specific, quantified, obligations to reduce emissions. That was intended to be for negotiation later. The Treaty also makes a distinction between developed and developing nations. It specifies that "developed country parties should take the lead". It specifically takes account of "the legitimate priority needs of developing countries for the achievement of sustained economic growth and eradication of poverty". The different positions of developed and developing countries were encapsulated in the Treaty, in the phrase, "common but differentiated responsibilities and respective capabilities".

All these provisions were necessary and appropriate. But they contained the seeds of subsequent difficulties in implementing the treaty. It has proved impossible to agree on any specific national targets through negotiation. It is true that developing nations need to give priority to economic development and it is reasonable that the richer nations, who historically created the problem and have the resources to address it, should go first. But one cannot get around the fact that most of the emissions, and all the growth of emissions, are now coming from the developing world. Developed nations, in making their commitments, understandably look over their shoulder to see if the developing countries are following.

The Kyoto Protocol, agreed in 1997, was the first attempt to negotiate national emissions targets. In this, the developed "Annex 1" nations agreed to legally binding limits on their emissions. Developing nations did not have specific limits, although these were expected in subsequent rounds. The Protocol included a Clean Development Mechanism whereby nations with specific limits could claim credits by investing in carbon-saving projects in other countries. There was also a carbon trading mechanism for trading between countries. The Protocol came into force in February 2005 when

55 Annex 1 countries had ratified. It was a diplomatic triumph marred, however, by the absence of the US and the limited commitment of China, the two most important players.

Under President Clinton, the US had played a leading role in negotiating the Protocol. However, in March 2001, President George Bush announced that the US would not ratify. He said, "The Kyoto Treaty would affect our economy in a negative way". China was not categorised as an Annex 1 participant and, accordingly, did not have an emissions target. So, neither of the two biggest emitters, the US and China, was bound to limits under the treaty.

There were two "commitment periods" from 2008 to 2012 and from 2012 to 2020. By the second period, a number of other major players, including Japan, Russia, and Canada, had dropped out. The Kyoto Protocol has now been superseded by the Paris Agreement, described in the following, which is based on "bottom-up" voluntary targets.

There were great hopes of a comprehensive new agreement on emissions levels at the Copenhagen Climate Summit in 2009, but, to the disappointment of many, negotiations broke down and the event was chaotic. At the last minute, President Obama and the Chinese Premier, with a small number of other leaders, drafted the "Copenhagen Accord". The Accord does not contain any specific national commitments to reduce emissions.

The Accord did, however, make the Climate Treaty's object of avoiding "dangerous ... interference with the climate system" more specific by setting the target of limiting global warming to below 2°C, a level that has since been criticised as not low enough. Also, at Copenhagen, the developed nations collectively promised to mobilise financial assistance to the developing world rising to $100 billion p.a. by 2020. Unfortunately, there was no breakdown of this sum between donor nations. No country had promised any specific sum, and this has turned out to be a problem.

There was considerable resentment among other countries that the Accord was drafted by such a small group. The Summit "took note" of the Accord without formally adopting it.

At the Durban Summit in 2011, agreement was reached, in principle, that a legally binding treaty, to include obligations on developing nations, should be negotiated by 2015 to come into effect by 2020.

In October 2014, preparing for the forthcoming 2015 Climate Summit in Paris, EU leaders agreed to cut emissions by at least 40% by 2030 compared to 1990.

In the following month, presidents Obama and Xi Jinping recognised, at a meeting in Washington, that climate change is "one of the greatest threats facing mankind". They agreed to work with other nations to make a success of the Paris Summit, and they each announced new national climate targets. President Obama said that the US would aim to reduce emissions by 26–28% in 2025 compared to 2005. President Xi Jinping said that China intended to achieve peak CO_2 emissions around 2030 with best efforts to peak earlier and that the share of non-fossil fuels in total energy supply would rise to around 20% by 2030. When the US and China come together, the "G2" is a potent force for driving global change. The prospects for world emissions reductions depend, in no small measure, on keeping this team in harness.

These major commitments by leading nations laid the foundation for the Paris Agreement which now provides the framework for climate diplomacy. Any attempt to negotiate national carbon quotas centrally, in other words, a "top-down" approach, was abandoned. Instead, each country was asked to make its own Nationally Determined Contribution (NDC). As the name implies, this is a firmly "bottom-up" approach in which decisions rest with individual sovereign nations. Following on from the commitments announced by the US, China, and the EU, almost every nation, and all the larger nations, announced their NDCs. India committed to reduce the energy intensity of GDP by 33–35% between 2005 and 2030.

The Paris Agreement, while benefiting from the support of the US and China, was undoubtedly a diplomatic triumph for the French hosts. The idea of imposing centrally negotiated emissions limits on participating countries was finally abandoned. That was pragmatic. The energy sector, and its associated emissions, are so fundamental to national prosperity that many countries, including the largest emitters, were unwilling to submit to such constraints. It was debatable whether the voluntary approach of the Paris Agreement fully met the Durban prospectus for a "legally binding" treaty. But it has provided a robust and practical framework that has been the basis for climate diplomacy ever since.

Under pressure from imminently threatened island states, the Paris Agreement, while repeating the 2°C target set in Copenhagen, added the intention to "pursue efforts to limit the temperature increase to 1.5°C".

However, the NDCs made around the Paris Climate Summit were nowhere near enough to contain global warming even to 2°C. According to the IEA, they were consistent with a continuing increase in emissions by about 10% to 2040, whereas 2°C would require a sharp fall of about a third. The IEA also judged that achieving 1.5°C would require that global emissions decline to net zero between 2040 and 2060.[27]

The Paris Summit commissioned the IPCC[28] to study the implications of aiming for 1.5°C. Its report,[29] published in 2018, said that climate change was "widespread, rapid, and intensifying", the temperature had already increased by 1°C and with present rates of emission, it was likely to reach 1.5°C between 2030 and 2032. It pointed to significant differences between the consequences of a 1.5°C rise in temperature and 2°C across a wide range of impacts and it said that in most of their models limiting climate change to the lower level would require net-zero CO_2 emissions by 2050. The Secretary General of the UN, Antonio Guterres, said that the report was a "code red for humanity".[30]

The National Contributions offered at the 2015 Paris Summit may not have been nearly sufficient to meet climate targets, but the intention was that they should be progressively improved, or "ratcheted up" with the first round of enhancement coming in five years' time. The 2020 Climate Summit, in Glasgow, had to be postponed because of the COVID-19 epidemic, so it did not take place until 2021. Most developed nations duly ratcheted up their Contributions.

The EU agreed to a new target of reducing greenhouse gas emissions by at least 55% between 1990 and 2030[31] (up from 40%). The US announced that it would aim for a 50–52% reduction by 2030 from 2005 (up from

26–28% by 2025).[32] India announced a 45% reduction in the intensity of greenhouse gases in its economy between 2005 and 2030 (up from 33–35%).[33]

However, to the disappointment of many, China did not announce any bringing forward of its existing overall target that its emissions will peak by 2030 and before if possible. Japan tightened its reduction target from 26% below the 2013 level by 2030 to 46% below. Russia tightened its target from 25% to 30% emissions reduction by 2030, but according to Climate Action Tracker, this is less than their current "business as usual" trajectory.

An important new development around the Glasgow Summit was that virtually all major nations set targets for reaching net-zero greenhouse gas emissions or net-zero CO_2 emissions at a later date. For most countries, including the US and the EU, this was 2050, but China and Russia have set their net zero dates at 2060 and India at 2070, significantly beyond 2050, the date around which the IPCC have said we need to reach net zero if we want to limit climate change to 1.5°C.

Recognising the weakness of the 2030 targets, the Summit agreed that nations should be asked to ratchet up their contributions in a year's time, not waiting another five years as before. However, the EU specifically declined to do so and there has been little improvement on the 2030 targets.[34] The Summit also agreed on the rules for international carbon trading, an important step that opens the door for businesses and governments to acquire credits by purchasing overseas emissions reductions.

There was also an agreement on methane emissions. Methane, also known as natural gas, is a more intensive agent of global warming than CO_2 although it does not stay in the atmosphere for so long. It should be a valuable product and only leaks into the atmosphere as a result of poor oil or gas field management or lack of infrastructure to bring it to market. An agreement to cut methane emissions by 3% by 2030 was signed by the EU, the US, and more than 100 other countries, but not by China, India, Russia, or Australia, who are among the largest emitters. An agreement to end deforestation was, however, signed by Brazil and Indonesia among others.

At the conclusion of the Glasgow Summit, a draft conclusion calling for the "phasing out" of coal was amended to "phasing down" at the request of major coal producers, including China and India. The UK Minister chairing the conference was reduced to tears.

In their November 2022 World Energy Outlook[35] the IEA note that "for the first time the collective government pledges and targets have been sufficient, if delivered in full and on time, to hold global warming to below 2°C". "However it is easier to make pledges than to implement them".

The IEA's "scenarios" illustrate how much work governments still have to do to follow through on their net zero commitments. In the net zero scenario world CO_2 emissions fall from 37 Gt today to 23 Gt in 2030 and, of course, net zero in 2050. But in their Stated Government Policies scenario emissions fall only to 35 Gt in 2030 and to 30 Gt by 2050. Essentially, emissions plateau before falling gradually. In that scenario the global temperature rises by 2.5° in 2100. If governments deliver fully on their announced pledges emissions are projected to decline to 31 Gt in 2030 and 12 Gt in 2050. In other words, most of the policies needed for achieving even the 2°C target are not yet in place. As the IEA has commented, "What is essential is for governments to turn their pledges into clear and credible policy actions and strategies today. Ambitions count for little if they are not implemented successfully".[36]

The IEA's analysis points to an important weakness of the Climate Treaty and the Paris process. Governments commit to targets that may be decades away, but there is no effective process for following up on progress towards meeting those targets and assessing whether the necessary policies are in place. This weakness is one of the issues for the international governance of climate mitigation that is discussed in the final chapter of this book.

The focus of the 2022 Climate Summit in Egypt was different from previous summits. Instead of focusing on emissions reduction targets, as previous summits have done, the agenda turned to the needs of developing nations. No major new climate targets were put forward. There was a power play by the developing nations, led by the G77 of developing nations plus China. The G77 was founded in 1964 to further the influence of developing nations, especially at the UN, and its membership has now increased to well over 100. China is not a member but has consistently supported the group.

At the summit, the developing nations made it an absolute condition of further progress that the developed nations should agree to set up a new fund to compensate them for "loss and damage" caused by climate change. Eventually, the developed nations, starting with the EU, gave in to this demand. There is to be a loss and damage fund. But everything about this fund remains to be decided, especially who will contribute and how much. The original proposal of the G77 plus China was that only the OECD nations, principally the US, Europe, and Japan should contribute. But these countries want to include other major emitters including China, Saudi Arabia, and Russia. China's role is likely to be salient, and it would be highly desirable for it to commit to contribute to the fund. The US government, for instance, will find it very difficult to win congressional support for paying into a loss and damage fund without it.

At a congressional hearing in July 2023, US climate envoy John Kerry said that "under no circumstances" would the US pay climate reparations to developing countries.[37] Perhaps that does not exclude a contribution to "loss and damage", but it certainly shows that the US has a very different view of the nature of this fund from that of the developing nations who have been pressing for it.

It is clearly essential that the developing world should share in the leadership of the climate effort. To that extent, a Climate Summit chaired by Egypt and specifically addressing concerns of developing nations was a welcome development. However, there was no effective follow-up to the call from the previous Glasgow Summit for another round of ratcheting up of emissions targets. It is a weakness of the UNFCCC Climate Summit process, which it shares with the G20, that the continuity of work on previously agreed initiatives remains hostage to the national priorities of each host nation as the summit chairmanship revolves.

It looks as though the next Climate Summit, COP 28, to be held in December 2023 and hosted by the United Arab Emirates, will also reflect the host nation's priorities. Not everyone is happy that it is to be chaired by the CEO of the Abu Dhabi National Oil Company (ADNOC). Al-Jaber is also the head of a renewable energy company, Masdar. He has called for the world to triple renewable energy generation by 2030 and more than double the production of low-carbon hydrogen. But critics worry that he calls for the reduction in emissions arising from oil and gas rather than reductions in oil and gas production itself and argues for the benefits of "least carbon-intensive oil and gas" in the energy transition.[38]

It looks as though COP 28, like COP 27 before it, will show a discontinuity from previous COPs hosted in Europe. But the West cannot expect to have complete control of the COP process. That is the world that we live in. Developing countries and even oil- and gas-producing countries will have to share the leadership. If COP 28 can accelerate investment in renewables, low-carbon hydrogen, energy efficiency, and the low-carbon use of fossil fuels through carbon capture and storage, those can all be important contributions.

Technology

Chart III shows how the three big fossil fuels, coal, oil, and gas continue to dominate the world energy supply. Turning this around represents a massive challenge.

Chart III.

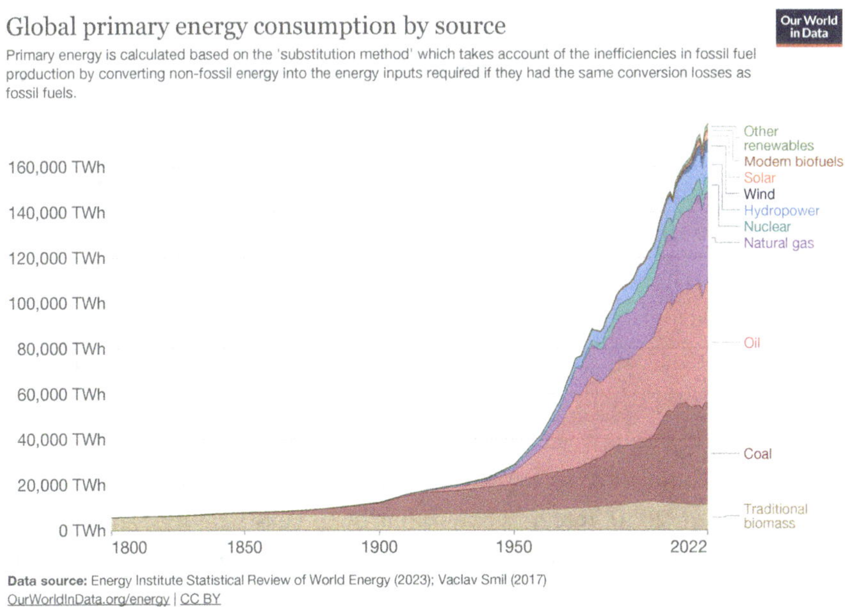

Technical progress determines the options for the future. So far, we have been fortunate with that. Some low-carbon technologies, especially wind, solar, and batteries have achieved spectacular cost reductions and, in the right circumstances, are now fully competitive. Some believe that these technologies alone, supported by flexible electric grids, can form the basis of low-carbon societies. A breakthrough in cheap grid-scale electric batteries, for instance, would be a big step in that direction. That is possible, but it's also a big risk. It is more likely that other technologies which have not achieved such big cost reductions, such as carbon storage, hydrogen, advanced biofuels, and nuclear power, will also be needed.

Governments and industry have invested heavily in the research, development, and demonstration of all these technologies but (with the partial exception of nuclear power) they have not yet taken the big financial risks or tough regulatory measures needed to achieve full-scale deployment. To have any chance of limiting global warming to 2°C, much less 1.5°C, governments now have to take some major risks in backing specific technologies to achieve full-scale deployment.

On the credit side, the fall in the cost of renewables has been spectacular, transforming the economics of energy transition, which now looks much more affordable than before.

The share of solar and wind in world electricity generation increased from 1.7% in 2010 to 11% in 2022, and by 2020, investment in these renewables was exceeding investment in upstream oil and gas. However, this increase contributed only about half of the growth in world electricity generation, so electricity from fossil fuels also continued to grow.

In 2023, the IEA expect around $2.8 trillion of global energy investment, of which $1.7 trillion will be in clean energy, including renewables, nuclear, grids, storage, and low-emission fuels.[39] That is impressive. And growth between 2021 and 2023 has been rapid. But that still isn't nearly enough. According to the IEA, the level of investment in renewables would have to approximately triple by 2030 to be consistent with net zero in 2050. Recent growth has been very heavily concentrated in the developed world plus China, and it has to spread more broadly across the developing world.

The crucial point is that we are still not investing enough in wind and solar power.

Other low-carbon technologies that are widely seen as having essential roles in a future low-carbon world have made much less progress. For instance, the importance of hydrogen, and the related chemical ammonia, has been recognised for decades, but we are still far away from large-scale deployment.

Hydrogen demonstrates, perhaps more than any other technology, the gap between ambition and achievement. Like electricity, hydrogen is an energy vector, and there is a wide range of possibilities for its production and use.

Hydrogen could meet domestic and industrial heating needs that are not so easily met by low-carbon electricity. Stored hydrogen used in gas turbines could provide backup, including seasonal backup, for variable renewables. Hydrogen can power vehicles, including heavy-duty vehicles less suitable for battery electric power, as well as ships and planes. However, none of these possibilities has yet taken off in a substantial way.

There are many projects around the world, especially in Europe, for producing low-carbon hydrogen and expanding its use. They are on a small scale so far, but the potential is immense.

Other technologies that have not taken off in the way that was hoped 10 or 20 years ago include carbon capture use and storage (CCUS) and advanced "cellulosic" biorefining that can make use of the woody parts of plants that cannot be used for food. Most low-carbon projections of world energy assume that CCUS will be needed on a large scale for three reasons. Conventional coal or gas power stations with their emissions captured and stored offer one of the few options available for reliable electricity generation to back up variable renewables, such as wind and solar. CCUS with biofuel-fired generation can extract CO_2 from the atmosphere and may be the most affordable way of doing so. And retrofitting existing coal or gas power stations with CCUS now appears the only alternative, consistent with meeting climate targets, to avoid premature retirement.

A lot of research is being carried out into CCUS, and there are a number of small-scale demonstration projects. But very few full-scale power stations have adopted the technology, and today it makes no significant contribution to reducing world emissions. Since CCUS is an add-on, it can never be competitive without government intervention, for instance through a carbon price, or until a sufficiently valuable use is found for bulk CO_2.

Lignocellulosic biorefineries were also hailed, 10 or 15 years ago, as low-carbon technologies of the future. They can transform the woody by-products of food crops, such as straw, into a wide range of liquid fuels and chemicals, and so greatly increase the potential for biofuels. There are several such refineries in existence, and research continues. But so far this technology also has failed to fulfil its early promise.

Nuclear power is arguably in the same category. Nuclear power does make a substantial contribution to the world energy supply today. After hydro, it is the largest source of low-carbon energy power. But, unlike wind and solar power, there has been no sharp reduction in costs. The building of new stations continues in the developing world, especially in China, but in the West, the future of nuclear power has been blighted by major delays and cost overruns in the construction of new stations. The war in Ukraine, and the search for energy security, may signal a turning point as the US, the EU, the UK, France, and even Japan pursue increasingly pro-nuclear policies, and even Germany may be reconsidering the closure of its remaining nuclear reactors. New concepts are under consideration, especially for smaller nuclear reactors. But it will take substantial government commitment to bring them into the mainstream.

So the performance of low-carbon technology thus far has to be regarded as patchy. Solar and wind energy have been spectacularly successful, but other promising technologies which we will almost certainly need have failed to come through as hoped.

Recent Developments

2023 Climate Summit

The climate summit held in November and December 2023 in Dubai was not the failure that some had feared. There was no overall tightening of targets but there were some important ad hoc announcements. More than 100 countries promised to triple the world's renewable capacity by 2030 and double the rate of energy efficiency. That is a significant step to doing "more of the same" as advocated in this book. But some of the most important players, such as China, India and South Africa, have not signed. Because these are collective targets, with no specific national commitments, it will be hard to hold individual governments to account.

Big oil companies, including all the Western major companies except Chevron, committed to achieving net zero methane emissions and to ending routine flaring by 2030. Again, an important step. However, the national oil companies of Russia, China, India, and Kuwait, who are amongst the biggest players, did not sign.

The Dubai Summit endorsed "transitioning away from fossil fuels in energy systems". This was hailed as a breakthrough by some but criticised by others because it somewhat watered down the reference to "phasing out fossil fuels" that was in earlier drafts of the conclusions. These headline pronouncements have some value but the real "transition" will depend on practical measures to reduce fossil fuel demand.

The Loss and Damage fund to support developing nations came into existence but, so far, with only modest finance. The "Global Stocktaking" conducted by the UNFCCC secretariat, intended as a highlight of the Summit, does not seem to have had much impact, which is a pity because it might have contributed to a more coherent outcome.

After some difficult wrangling, it was agreed that Azerbaijan, another oil state, will host the 2024 summit. This is not a disaster; it will probably result in more worthwhile ad hoc commitments but no comprehensive tightening of the screw on carbon emissions.

Financial and Political Headwinds

While investment in low carbon energy has continued at a rapid pace there have been significant headwinds for the green agenda. High interest rates and supply chain difficulties have slowed, and in some cases reversed, the trend of declining costs for low carbon energy. After a year in which its renewable power auctions received no bids, the UK government has had to increase the price offered for offshore wind from £44 to £77 per MWh, and is under pressure to renegotiate some existing deals. However, inflation is currently declining rapidly in Europe and the US, so hopefully high interest will turn out to be a temporary phenomenon.

In the political sphere, the difficulty of winning public acceptance for low carbon policies has become increasingly evident. The UK government has significantly backtracked on green regulation following a local election which seems to have been swayed by a public backlash. Most significantly the date for ending the sale of petrol and diesel cars has been pushed forward from 2030 to 2035. Considering the longevity of modern vehicles, 2035 seems about the last possible date that could be consistent with net zero in 2050. There has also been some relaxation in plans to move away from gas central heating. Prime Minister Sunak said, "We are going to make progress towards net zero but were are going to do that in a proportionate and pragmatic way that doesn't unnecessarily give people more hassle and more cost in their lives".[40] It looks as though both the main parties in the forthcoming general election will be anxious to reassure the public that green regulation is not going to impose significant cost or inconvenience. The Labour party, which is a strong favourite to take power, is back peddling on a promise to spend £28 billion p.a. on green policies. There have been similar signs of public resistance to the cost and inconvenience of green regulation in Europe, especially Germany, and in the US.

Conclusion

Summarising the state of play, on the plus side, the structural trends of economic development are helping to reduce the level of emissions in the developed OECD countries and now slow the growth of emissions in China. The spectacular progress and cost reductions of wind and solar power are making low-carbon transition much more affordable. Public opinion increasingly recognises the urgency of the situation. So does business, with more major companies reporting on their transition strategies, and the rapid development of green financing. City and provincial governments have become active, and there is now a global framework for government action. Virtually, all governments have announced low-carbon targets, and now, if you credit commitments that are several decades into the future, the sum of these commitments seems just about sufficient to contain global warming to 2°C. There is no denying that all this adds up to impressive progress.

On the other hand, as of today, global emissions continue their remorseless rise. That is in contrast to the sharp reduction that is needed urgently to meet climate targets. Governments have not yet adopted the policies that are required to make that happen. Indeed, there has been a worrying trend that major new commitments are tending towards the longer-term future, to 2050 and beyond. Investment in renewables has been impressive, but it is still well below what is needed, and other low-carbon technologies, such as hydrogen, biofuels, and CCUS are lagging behind.

We need a lot more of the things that we are doing already, especially investing in renewables and promoting energy efficiency. That is Key Policy No. 1, and it is the first fundamental of low-carbon energy policy. We may, or may not, be on the cusp of a true energy revolution. The future of the planet hangs on that.

Chapter 2

Technology: Creating and Using the Right Tools

Key Policy No. 2.

Renewable electricity will be at the heart of the low-carbon world of the future. But for net zero, we also need technologies that can fill in for the variability of renewables and provide energy for other major CO_2-emitting sectors that are difficult to electrify. These include major industries, such as steel and cement, as well as aviation, shipping, and heavy vehicles. There are a variety of promising low-carbon options, including hydrogen, carbon capture use and storage, and advanced nuclear. Such is the scale of the need that probably all these technologies will be needed. However, there is still uncertainty about their potential and there may be winners and losers. Governments will need to invest heavily and accept some well-considered risks. This is Key Policy No. 2.

Introduction

As Chart IV shows, fossil fuels still account for nearly 80% of world energy. Dispensing with them requires a fundamental turn-around in our energy supply, in which they are largely replaced by solar, wind, biofuels, and nuclear with the emissions from almost all the remaining fossil energy sequestered.

Chart IV.

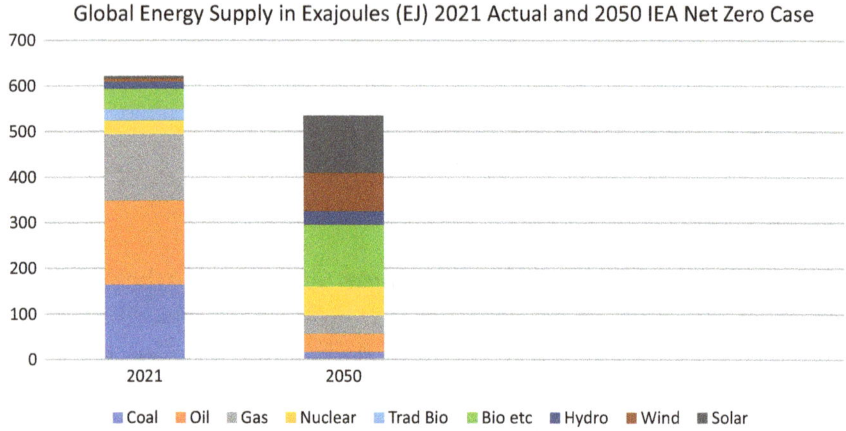

Source: Data taken from the IEA's World Energy Outlook 2022.

The chart also shows that to achieve net zero in 2050, the IEA believes that, notwithstanding continuing economic growth, world energy demand will need to be significantly less than it is today. It projects a 60% reduction in the energy intensity of the global economy, making energy efficiency and other ways of reducing energy demand the most important factors in reducing CO^2 emissions. As the IEA has said, "No other energy resource can compete with energy efficiency as a solution to the energy affordability, security of supply, and climate change crises".[41]

The technical progress of the past few decades has meant that a revolution in energy supply technology is not totally implausible. But first, we will have to get some key technologies over the hurdle of mass deployment and greatly increase the penetration of technologies that are already deployed. That will require bold action by governments and a certain amount of good fortune with technical progress.

The costs of wind and solar electricity generation have declined spectacularly in recent decades. And deployment has accelerated on an extraordinary scale. It may, now, be just about sufficient to match the rapid growth in electricity demand, but it is not yet sufficient to bring about a reduction in generation from coal and gas.

Fossil fuels are beginning to look unattractive, not only for environmental reasons but also because, based on extractive industries, they cannot match the cost reductions of renewables. It may well be that, eventually, renewable alternatives are set largely to replace coal, oil, and gas, in any case, even without government intervention. But this is not happening anything like fast enough to contain global warming to safe levels.

There are still big gaps in our tool box. We are without competitive low-carbon options for heating, industry, aviation, and shipping, sectors that together account for about a third of world emissions. And the variability of wind and solar generation is still a serious barrier to really high levels of reliance on them for electric power.

If we were aiming for, say, a 70% reduction in carbon emissions, we could say that we already have affordable technologies that can get us there even if deployment is far from assured. But 100% is a much tougher proposition altogether.

Real uncertainty remains about the range of technologies that will be needed to get us to net zero. A big breakthrough in electric battery technology would change the landscape for electricity supply and for vehicles. Big reductions in the cost of producing hydrogen from water by electrolysis could open the door for hydrogen in various chemical combinations to power ships, aeroplanes, and heavy vehicles and possibly contribute to reliable electricity supply. Further improvements in the cost and performance of all these technologies are to be expected with continuing research and development and increased deployment. But major breakthroughs cannot be taken for granted.

Unlike wind and solar, some of the other technologies that seem most significant are not yet on pathways to mass deployment and rapid cost reduction. These include nuclear power, capture and storage of emissions, a whole range of possible uses of hydrogen, and other options that might eventually enable us to store electricity in bulk over long periods.

Very large investments are needed in these technologies to enable them to deliver their potential, even though it is still not certain which of them will be the big winners. Governments will have to be brave and take risks. If they get it right, the potential rewards are immense.

The growth of renewables and electric vehicles in the West has been based, to a considerable degree, on the import of low-cost components and materials from China. For instance, 70% of all photovoltaic modules were manufactured in China in 2020. The next biggest manufacturers were Vietnam with 7% and South Korea with 5%. The US contributed 3% and Europe 2%. China is even more dominant in the supply of specialist materials and components. That trade with China is now threatened by geopolitical tensions and the erosion of trust. We live in an imperfect world. The state of relations between China and the West will have a material impact on the progress of low-carbon technology, at least in the medium term.

This chapter reviews energy efficiency and the five main sectors contributing to CO_2 emissions, the technologies available to eliminate them, and the government policies that are needed to achieve this. The five sectors are, in descending order of global emissions:

- electricity generation,
- heating and cooling of buildings,
- industry,
- road transport,
- aviation,
- shipping.

This ranking varies greatly from country to country. Hot countries do not have to heat buildings, but they may have a rapidly growing demand for air conditioning. For countries with high reliance on hydropower or nuclear power, emissions from electricity generation may be much less significant. For the UK, a "post- industrial" society, emissions from industry are much less significant than those from transport and heating buildings. In China, industry is the biggest emitter.

Some key technologies with multiple applications are dealt with substantially in the section on electricity, which is why it is much the longest. The following sections deal only with points relevant to other specific uses.

Energy Efficiency

If we had a magic wand that could quickly convert all sources of energy to zero carbon then energy efficiency would not matter for climate change. That is far from the case. The transition will be costly, difficult, and uncertain. Improving energy efficiency can reduce the size of the problem. Indeed, as noted above, it's the most important factor. Energy efficiency is already making a big contribution. For instance, energy efficiency gains approximately halved the rate of global energy demand growth between 2016 and 2021.

Unfortunately, the trends are not favourable. World improvements in energy efficiency averaged just over 2% p.a. between 2011 and 2015 but only 1.4% p.a. between 2016 and 2019. They fell further in 2020 and 2021 before rebounding somewhat in 2022. The IEA judges that efficiency needs to improve by 4% p.a. between 2020 and 2030 for the world to be on course for net zero in 2050. At that rate, it would reduce emissions by about one-third of what they would otherwise have been in 2030.[42]

Major contributions to energy efficiency come from industry, buildings, appliances and vehicles. For industry, the main issues are right-sizing pumps and boilers and boiler efficiency, insulation, and energy management. For buildings, they include building regulations and drives to improve insulation and central heating boiler efficiency in existing homes and offices. Also important are regulations to improve the energy efficiency of appliances and lighting, and regulation of vehicles to improve fuel efficiency and ultimately to promote electric cars and vans.

This is a broad prospectus. Energy efficiency is not the most glamorous of climate measures, but it is often the most cost-effective. It requires constant attention on the part of government, industry, and consumers.

Energy efficiency suffers from the fact that it is not a commodity that can easily be marketed and sold. There are energy service companies that invest in mainly business efficiency measures and then take a share of the savings in energy costs as their returns. Some of these companies have been successful, but they all face the challenge of measuring fuel savings against the constantly changing activities and varying energy demands of many organisations.

The problems of persuading domestic consumers to invest in energy efficiency are well illustrated by a scheme launched in 2013 by the UK government known as the Green Deal. The Green Deal was intended to address the fact that the UK has a high proportion of older homes and one of the least efficient housing stocks in Europe. Homes are responsible for more than a quarter of the UK's energy demand.

The scheme offered householders a government-sponsored appraisal of home energy efficiency measures. It also offered loans to put these measures into effect. The cost of servicing these loans was to be included in future utility bills. It was expected that the savings from reduced fuel consumption would more than outweigh the cost of servicing the loans, leaving the householder better off overall. The scheme had its merits. Government sponsorship was expected to reassure householders about the quality of the work to be carried out and the calculation that they would be better off overall. The inclusion of debt service in energy bills was expected to enhance the security of the debt enabling it to be financed at a competitive interest rate.

Householders were unpersuaded. Very few of them took up the scheme and it was cancelled within a few years. Energy efficiency was not high enough on the public's list of priorities to motivate them to enter a complicated financial deal and run the risk of some home disruption. Perhaps they did not trust the government.

Improving the energy efficiency of homes is just one of many practical things that people can do to reduce carbon emissions. Buy smaller cars, cut back on air travel, use public transport, turn down the thermostat, and recycle used products. Business also has many options. Use less steel in manufacturing, including cars, and construction, use less cement and less carbon-intensive cement mixes, cut down on packaging, and reduce business flying. Not all of these are strictly efficiency gains, but they all reduce carbon emissions.

Government plays a major role in regulating and incentivising energy efficiency measures. But there is also a wide range of options for reducing energy demand and carbon emissions that can be adopted with only marginal care and inconvenience, and which do not depend on government action. It all comes down to raising climate change on the list of priorities of the public and of business and of pointing out the relevance of their own actions. It may not be as popular as fulminating against the government or distant corporations but it's a key role for opinion influencers.

Electricity Generation

Nearly 40% of global emissions from energy are due to electricity generation. Demand for electricity is growing rapidly around the world, at about double the rate of growth of energy as a whole, and almost all commentators expect that electricity will be the backbone of the low-carbon economies of the future. Electricity is flexible and clean at the point of use. It is vital to the expanding world of information, communications, and entertainment, and for air conditioning. Its role is expected to increase further with the adoption of electric vehicles and heat pumps to provide domestic and commercial heating. In the short term the costs of wind and solar power now seem to be stabilising. Whether cost reductions will resume now depends on the cost of materials and on relations between the West and China, as a major supplier. These topics are considered further in Chapter 5.

Renewables

The progress of renewable energy has been spectacular. The costs of photovoltaic solar modules have fallen by about 90% in the last 10 years and of wind turbines by more than 50%. In many situations, wind and solar are now the lowest-cost options for electricity generation. According to the IEA, solar power now costs $55 per MWh in Europe and onshore wind $50 per MWh, with the prospect of substantial further reductions. Coal costs

$170 and combined cycle gas $110. Nuclear costs $150. The figures vary in different parts of the world and fluctuate with coal and gas prices. But in most situations, renewables are now the cheapest source of electricity supply and the gap in relation to coal and gas is increasing.

This is a fundamental transformation in energy supply. The IEA is now projecting that almost 95% of the world's new electricity generating capacity over the next five years will be in renewables and 50% in solar photovoltaics alone.[43] Batteries have also shown rapid improvements in cost and performance, and this is transforming the outlook for electric vehicles.

The great majority of solar power comes from photovoltaic cells (PV). A much smaller share is generated from Concentrated Solar Power (CSP) in which the sun's rays are concentrated, by mirrors, on a boiler that heats molten salt. CSP is generally more costly than PV but has the advantage that energy can be stored in its molten salt boilers.

There is a long way to go. In 2022, solar and wind power together accounted for only 11% of world generation, compared to 36% for coal, 22% for gas, 15% for hydro, and 9% for nuclear. However, wind and solar are growing much faster than the other sources.

Most visions of a net zero future rely heavily on renewables. For instance in the IEA's net zero by 2050 scenario, solar and wind contribute nearly 70% of world electricity supply and electricity contributes almost 50% of world energy consumption.[44] The other big contributors are hydro, bioenergy, and nuclear power. By that time, solar PV and wind, both onshore and offshore, are expected to be the cheapest sources of power, by far. This applies in virtually all parts of the world, with solar energy especially cheap in China and India. Wind and light conditions vary, as well as access to suitable land or offshore sites. However, the potential is abundant in most regions. A big part of the challenge, therefore, is to find low-carbon solutions to the energy needs that cannot easily be met with wind- and solar-generated electricity, including backup for intermittency.

Intermittency is not a problem for a mature grid so long as renewables account for around 25% of generation or less. The rest of the system can adapt at a modest cost. The problem arises as renewables become dominant. The decline in the cost of batteries means that they are now able to handle, cost-effectively, relatively short-term imbalances between renewable electricity supply and demand. For instance, in California, or much of India, the peak of solar generation is a fairly good match to the peak of electricity demand for air conditioning, except that this demand continues for several hours after the sun has gone down. Electric batteries are suitable for meeting that gap.

The problem arises from longer term or seasonal imbalances. For instance, in the UK and much of Europe, it is possible to have periods of weeks or even months of limited wind and heavy cloud cover. The cost of storing a significant share of the total electricity supply over these periods is prohibitive. Breakthroughs in battery technology, or in a whole range of other options being explored may yet solve this problem, but that isn't in sight today.

Security of Electricity Supply

Actual power failure can be catastrophic in a modern economy. So much of the economy, of communications, and the safety and security of citizens depend on continuous power supply. However advanced grid design gives the operator a better range of options short of total power failure. Some large industrial users can be disconnected at significant economic cost but without lasting damage. If that is not enough, short predicted outages can be spread across regions. These are not attractive options, but they may be appropriate to deal with supply shortages that would be very rare events.

Part of the solution may come from sophisticated grids and demand-side contributions. Smart metres enable electricity suppliers to charge different rates at different times of the day according to the cost and availability of supply. Customers, both domestic and industrial, may vary their demand accordingly. Smart appliances may adjust automatically. As electric vehicles become more usual, their batteries may contribute to this flexibility.

This isn't happening yet and it remains to be seen how willing customers, and especially domestic customers, will be to adapt. At present, customers can have electricity at a standard rate whenever they want it. That is beginning to look like a luxury that we cannot afford. In the future, they will have to accept that, for instance, running a washing machine at a time of high electricity demand and low wind will be prohibitively expensive. Similarly, they may have to accept limitations on when they can charge electric cars at a reasonable cost and perhaps even allow the grid operator to take power from car batteries at times of stress. All this will be presented to consumers as a positive opportunity to manage and reduce their own electricity costs. They may take some persuading. There is a need for large-scale pilot schemes to test how all this might work.

Another option is to extend the grid to cover wider regions. The sun may not be shining, or the wind may not be blowing here, but all may be well if the grid is connected to other regions where conditions are different or which are more reliant on other sources, such as hydro or nuclear power. There are certainly economic benefits from arbitrage between regions with different cost structures. Grids across Europe and the US are becoming more connected partly for this reason. There are proposals to connect North Africa with Europe. China is promoting a grand plan, perhaps fanciful in the immediate future, for a mega grid that would connect the whole of Asia.

There are obvious risks in becoming too reliant on supplies that are beyond the control of national regulators. The dependence of the European Union on Russian gas provided a cautionary tale in 2022. And wind or solar conditions, say between the UK and Germany, may turn out not to be so very different. When one country's grid calls up another in an hour of need, they may find that the other country is in just as much trouble.

These options can increase the flexibility of power systems and make it possible to rely on wind and solar to a larger extent. The exact share will depend on local and regional conditions and on technical progress.

But in all probability, in most parts of the world, a significant contribution from more reliable sources of power will be needed to provide backup.

Initially gas may provide this backup. The gas stations already exist and they can be operated flexibly, although there is a cost to keeping them maintained and ready to run for only occasional use. They are, however, CO_2 emitters.

To achieve net zero, low-carbon alternatives to gas will eventually have to be found. There are three technologies that already supply reliable low-carbon electricity on a large scale: hydropower, nuclear power, and bioenergy. Also, geothermal power, although it is not a big player in global generation, is well established and a major contributor in some countries with favourable geology.

Hydropower

Today, hydropower is the world's largest generator of low-carbon electricity, contributing 15% of world electricity generation in 2022. Hydropower dominates in countries such as Norway and Brazil. Canada, the US, and Russia all have substantial capacity, but China has by far the greatest. Hydropower is the perfect backup for variable renewables because water in the reservoir is, effectively, stored energy that can be used at short notice and at any time. However, climate change may affect the pattern of rainfall and therefore the availability of hydropower. This is a growing concern, for instance in China, after the hot and dry summer of 2022.

Not all countries have suitable geography for hydropower. Even where opportunities exist, new schemes are often controversial because of the need, for really large projects, to create reservoirs by flooding valleys. Hydropower will continue to play an important role in world energy, but its growth is likely to be restricted.

Nuclear Power

Nuclear power is already the world's second-largest source of low-carbon electricity, after hydro. It contributes 9% of electricity world-wide and 20% in the developed OECD world. If existing stations retire without replacement, that will be a major setback for the low-carbon transition. In their net zero scenario, the IEA estimates that double today's capacity will be needed by 2050.

Nuclear power capacity grew rapidly in the West during the 1970s, when it seemed destined to dominate world electricity supply. There is a cautionary tale here for policymakers: the future is not always what we expect. The growth of nuclear power came to a grinding halt in the US and most of Europe in the 1980s as a result of competition from cheap natural gas, the combined cycle gas turbine, and safety fears following the accident at Chernobyl in 1986.

France and Japan, both countries lacking in natural energy resources, persevered with nuclear power, as did South Korea. France now gets 75% of its electricity from nuclear power and as a result emits less than half the CO_2 in relation to GDP that the OECD average, well below the UK or Germany.

Following the accident at Fukushima in Japan in 2011, all the Japanese reactors were closed. Only a minority have since reopened. As a result, Japan has become increasingly dependent on imports of liquefied natural gas from Australia and elsewhere. Germany vowed to close all its remaining reactors after Fukushima. France announced plans to moderate its dependence on nuclear power in favour of renewables.

However, there has been a more positive story on life extensions. Many existing stations in the US and Europe have had their lives extended to 60 or even 80 years, which helps explain why nuclear power remains so significant today.

The near-universal commitment to net zero among major nations following the Glasgow Climate Summit and the turmoil in gas markets as a result of the war in Ukraine have changed the landscape of international energy policy. Nuclear power should now be in pole position to benefit. Governments are looking for secure, reliable, low-carbon electricity and that is what nuclear power provides *par excellence*. All over the developed world, we have seen sharp swings in policy towards nuclear power. Most spectacularly, the Japanese government has announced plans for reviving its nuclear power industry, even while many reactors are still closed down today, following Fukushima. California is reconsidering the closure of the Diablo Canyon power station. France has reversed a policy of steadily reducing its dependence on nuclear power and President Macron has now said that he intends to order six new European Pressurised Reactors (EPRs), with options for a further eight. The UK is pressing ahead with plans for a second EPR. South Korea has reversed its plans to phase out nuclear power, and even Germany is reconsidering the closure of its remaining nuclear stations. In the US, nuclear power qualifies, along with renewables, for massive incentives under the Inflation Reduction Act, and, after a tussle with Germany, the European Union has designated nuclear power as a "sustainable" energy source which qualifies for government support.

However, the nuclear power industry in the West will have to overcome some serious difficulties to take advantage of this change of fortune. Its recent record of nuclear construction has been dire. There are two currently available full-scale reactor designs: the Westinghouse AP1000 and the German/French EPR. Of the two AP1000 stations that were under construction in the US, one was cancelled in mid-stream as costs spiralled, and the other, at Voghtle, has suffered huge delays and cost increases. In Europe, the two EPRs at Flamanville in France and Olkiluoto in Finland have also suffered massive overruns in time and cost. Westinghouse filed for bankruptcy and the French constructor Areva had to be rescued by EDF and the French government. It isn't a pretty picture.

A 2020 study by MIT assessed the reasons for the severe cost overruns in US nuclear power plant construction since 1970.[45] Most of them were due to "soft costs" of engineering, administration, and supervision rather than "hard costs" of materials and labour. The main "high-level" causes were design changes following R&D and "interference" by on-site safety personnel in the construction process. The study suggests that construction progress became bogged down for these reasons, leading to poor morale and poor productivity overall. Surprisingly, the study says that it may be better to start from a new design that it is possible to stick to, rather than starting from existing designs that are more vulnerable to modification for safety or other reasons.

It is hard to believe that there are no benefits from repeating existing designs. For instance, the constructors of the two identical reactors at Hinkley Point C are claiming significant efficiency improvements in building the second reactor. The moral seems to be that these benefits are lost if design "upgrading" is allowed, especially during the construction period.

When the UK ordered a huge EPR nuclear power station in 2017, it seemed like a big risk, taking account of the poor construction record of

EPR rectors so far. Thomas Piquemal, the finance director of EDF, the main contractor, resigned in protest.[46]

Meanwhile, in China, two AP1000 stations and two EPRs have been successfully constructed with only limited delays and are now in operation. China, India, and Pakistan, where much of the future growth of energy demand will be concentrated, have continued with substantial programmes of new nuclear construction, though not on the scale of their investment in renewables.

Russia also has a major nuclear power industry. Nuclear power contributed nearly 20% of Russia's electricity in 2019. Russia is the most successful nation in the export of nuclear power stations with their state nuclear energy corporation, Rosatom, claiming $133 billion of export orders in 2017. Mostly, these will be versions of the VVER-1000, a Russian-designed PWR. Russia is exporting to China, India, Turkey, Iran, Egypt, and Bangladesh, among other countries.[47]

People worry about the safety of nuclear power, waste management, and the risk of proliferation of nuclear materials and expertise. These are all legitimate concerns. Most people would prefer to rely on renewables. But renewables are not always available. For modern, well-managed, and well-regulated nuclear power stations, the risks are low and certainly much less than those of global warming.

The big drawback with nuclear power is cost, especially in the light of recent construction experience in the West. To order the nuclear power station now under construction, Hinkley Point C, the UK government had to guarantee an inflation-linked price of £92.50 per MWh of generation at a time when offshore wind was costing £57.50. The prices are not directly comparable because offshore wind is intermittent. Nevertheless, on this basis, nuclear power looks expensive. The IEA estimates the cost of nuclear power in 2050 in Europe, the US, China, and India at two or three times the cost of solar PV or onshore wind.

A nuclear power station requires a large initial investment and has a long construction period. Then, it should operate for up to 80 years with operating and fuel costs that are much lower than for a coal or gas plant. Recent experience in the West shows that the commercial risk of ballooning construction costs is substantial. What price of the electricity is needed to repay the investment cost? That depends almost entirely on the discount rate applied to future earnings or, in the commercial world, the rate of return required by the investing business.

The UK government had to guarantee an inflation-linked price of £92.50 per MWh for 30 years to float Hinkley Point C. That was calculated to give EDF, the main developer, a return of around 9% p.a. on their investment, assuming the success of the project. That is not excessive considering the commercial risks involved. However, the UK's Parliamentary watchdog[48] has pointed out that if the project was financed at the government's rate of borrowing, which was around 2% p.a. at the time, the necessary price could be as low as £27.50 per MWh or even zero because power generated after the 30-year price guarantee period might more than pay for the project. Government borrowing costs have risen sharply since then, but it is likely to remain true that governments can borrow at rates significantly below those required by private companies undertaking projects with significant business risk.

If Hinkley Point C can be built successfully, that will greatly reduce the construction risks of a sister project now proposed at Sizewell, also in the UK. It may be more realistic for electricity consumers to accept those risks. In other words, the project can be at least partially socialised and financed at a much lower cost than Hinkley Point C. That is what the UK government is aiming to do.

Governments have to regulate the safety of nuclear power and the management of waste. They are also involved, through complex international treaties,[49] in insurance against catastrophic nuclear risks. Under the Vienna and Paris conventions, nuclear operators have "no-fault" liability for the consequences of nuclear accidents. However, governments have the obligation to step in should the contribution of the operator be insufficient. The industry depends on public acceptance of those risks. All this underlines the fact that nuclear power, more than other sources of electricity, is essentially a social undertaking, justified only as part of a broad government strategy on energy security.

Hinkley Point C is expected to cost £25 billion and will be at least 8 years in construction. There is now a push for smaller reactor designs that do not pose such "lumpy" financing hurdles. The aim is to produce more of the components in factories and simplify the work required on site. Ideally, there will be a run of identical orders leading to increased reliability and reduced cost.

There is also a wide range of next-generation nuclear reactors under development around the world. The broad aims are to improve safety, for instance, through passive safety systems, and to simplify construction. Sodium-cooled Fast Reactors (SFRs) and Very High Temperature Reactors (VHTRs) are among the most advanced designs. The SFR offers the opportunity to recycle and reuse spent fuel. Russia, for instance, is planning to make fast reactors with fuel recycling the basis of its future nuclear industry. The VHTR has a large graphite core that makes it much more stable in the event of an accident than the Pressurised Water Reactors (PWRs) that we mainly use today. Ironically, these were all technologies that were being developed in the UK in the 1970s and 1980s, before being overtaken by the "dash for gas".

Probably, these smaller and more advanced reactors represent the future of nuclear power. The US, China, France, Japan, and India all have significant development programmes. Rolls-Royce has made a proposal for a smaller but otherwise conventional PWR design that could be operating by 2030. Rolls-Royce already has experience in making smaller nuclear reactors for submarines. However, there are other, competing, proposals.

In July 2023, the UK government announced a "massive revival of nuclear power" in the form of a competition that "could result in billions of pounds of public and private sector investment in Small Modular Reactor (SMR) projects in the UK". It doesn't appear that the Treasury is yet signed up to the scale of finance that this would imply.

Meanwhile, it looks as though the first of today's latest full-scale designs, the French/German EPR, and the US-designed Westinghouse APR1000 are finally struggling to completion. Proving new designs and winning safety clearance is a time-consuming process. Probably, the new advanced designs are at least a decade away. The projected cost benefits are not yet proven. The nuclear power industry has been plagued by constant changes in design, which have been a major cause of "first-of-a-kind" construction problems. For the time being, it makes good sense to repeat order the existing designs that, hopefully, have at last overcome their teething problems. Love the one you're with, at least for a while.

Governments should also persevere in their support for smaller and advanced reactor designs that can be repeat ordered, leading to reliable construction and declining costs. At that stage, private finance may flow into the industry. That may be the future of nuclear power in the longer term.

Bioenergy

Bioenergy contributed about 2% of world electricity generation in 2022, making it the largest low-carbon contributor after renewables, hydro, and nuclear. The sources of biofuels are diverse, but municipal waste, forestry, sugarcane waste, and wood chips and pellets are the most important.

The availability of suitable feedstock from environmentally sustainable sources varies from region to region. The gathering of low-grade agricultural residues, such as straw, can be expensive. The use of wood pellets from managed forests is controversial. Although the CO_2 released as the pellets are burnt has been absorbed from the atmosphere as the trees grew, it has been argued that if the trees had been left to mature, they would have retained more CO_2 for a period that is long enough to help ease the climate crisis.

The use of biofuels for electricity generation also has to be weighed against alternative uses for the feedstock. As discussed in the following, biofuels may be essential for the de-carbonisation of aviation and possibly shipping and heavy trucks.

Bioenergy can provide flexible electricity generation to complement variable renewables. It can be blended with coal as a transitional carbon reduction measure. Most importantly, bioenergy with carbon capture and storage, known as BECCS, is today the most cost-effective way of removing CO_2 from the atmosphere, in other words of achieving negative carbon emissions. It is much less costly to capture CO_2 that is concentrated in the emissions of a power station than to remove it from the air. We can never eliminate CO_2 emissions altogether and now that governments are setting targets of net zero, it is inevitable that negative carbon emissions will be needed.

Geothermal

Geothermal energy, extracting heat from the earth's crust, is well established as a means of power generation in many countries. However, world generating capacity, of about 15GW, is modest, equal to about one-fifth of the UK's total capacity. It does not play a big part in most countries' net zero plans. Geothermal power is most economic where hot rocks are closest to the surface, often in earthquake zones, but there is potential to develop it almost anywhere at a greater cost.

The above has covered all the major sources of low-carbon electricity generation currently available. All other low-carbon sources account for less than 1% of total generation together. However, two of these sources, hydrogen and fossil fuels with captured emissions, have been the subject of intense research and development. They have both reached the stage of full-scale demonstration, are widely regarded as essential for achieving net zero, and, hopefully, are now on a rapidly rising trajectory.

Hydrogen

"Hope springs eternal in the human breast," wrote poet Alexander Pope.[50] Hydrogen, with various associated chemicals, can store, transport, and deliver energy that is free of greenhouse gas emissions at the point of use. It could overcome the limitations of electricity, which is expected to be the main vector for low-carbon energy in the future. However, today, hydrogen is part of the problem. Its production, for use in the chemical industry, is a significant source of CO_2 emissions. Determined government action is required first to meet the existing demand for hydrogen from low-carbon sources and then to stimulate a larger market for low-carbon hydrogen, combined with significant technical progress.

The universe is largely made of hydrogen. It isn't in short supply. Hydrogen contains three times as much energy as petrol by weight but, even in liquefied form, only one quarter by volume. Hydrogen gas contains about one-third of the energy of natural gas by volume.

Today, hydrogen is mainly used in oil refining and in the manufacture of ammonia (NH_3), the main fertiliser that sustains world agriculture. It is generally produced by steam "reforming" of natural gas, a process which currently emits about 830 million tonnes of CO_2 p.a., about 2% of the world's total.

Options exist for producing hydrogen with much reduced, or no, CO_2 emissions. Hydrogen produced from fossil fuels, the main practice today, is known as "grey" hydrogen. Most, but not quite all, of the carbon emissions can be captured and stored, and if that technology is added, the product is known as "blue" hydrogen. However, hydrogen can also be produced by electrolysis of water. Provided that the electricity is generated from renewables, there are no CO_2 emissions. This is known as "green" hydrogen. From an environmental perspective, this is the most exciting prospect because green hydrogen could be stored during periods of abundant renewable generation and then used to generate power through gas turbines when renewable power is short. In other words, it could play a significant role in solving the problem of intermittence.

However, today, in 2023, it is much more expensive to produce hydrogen by electrolysis from renewables than by reforming natural gas, \$3–8 per kg of hydrogen compared to \$0.5–1.7, according to the IEA.[51]

Production of blue and green hydrogen is starting from a very low level but is increasing rapidly. According to the IEA, global capacity of electrolysers doubled over the last five years to reach just over 300 MW by mid-2021. If all the projects now in the early stages of development are realised, global hydrogen supply from electrolysers could reach more than 8 Mt by 2030. While significant, this is still well below the 80 Mt required by that year in the pathway to net-zero CO_2 emissions by 2050 set out in the IEA Roadmap for the Global Energy Sector. Similarly, projects now in prospect for producing hydrogen from fossil fuels with CCUS could produce 9 Mt p.a. by 2030. For comparison, about 90 Mt of hydrogen is used today.[52]

Hydrogen can be stored in salt caverns or, most probably, in liquefied form above ground. It can be converted into electricity in gas turbines or fuel cells. Hydrogen has many other potential uses other than for electricity generation, for instance, in transport and for heating, and these are discussed in the following.

The electrolysis of water is a well-proven technology, but it is still at an early stage of deployment. There are reasonable hopes that big cost reductions can be achieved with further research and development and wider use. The IEA believes that with sufficient investment, in regions with low-cost renewable electricity supply the cost of green hydrogen could become competitive with grey hydrogen by 2030, opening the door to mass adoption.

The disadvantages of hydrogen are its low energy content by volume and the fact that it can only be liquefied at a very low temperature. However, it is much easier to liquefy, and therefore to transport, in the form of ammonia, a product of hydrogen and nitrogen with chemical formula NH_3, that is in very general use as fertiliser. Hydrogen, together with captured CO_2, can also be converted into methanol (CH_3OH), a stable liquid fuel that can be stored and used like petrol. Methanol's environmental qualities are similar to those of biofuels. The carbon captured for the manufacture of methanol is then emitted when it is burnt, leading to no net emissions. Italy and Germany are pressing that when the EU commission bans new internal combustion engines in 2035, an exception should be made for engines running on e-fuels, such as methanol. That seems a reasonable thing to do provided that, as the Commission seem to fear, this isn't a loophole for the continued production of cars that will actually run on petrol.

Imported hydrogen could provide low-carbon electricity for countries with limited renewables. The world's first shipment of liquefied blue hydrogen left Australia for Japan in February 2022. Saudi Arabia has some of the cheapest solar power in the world and has said that hydrogen manufactured from renewables will play a significant part in its plans to diversify from oil and gas. In August 2020, Saudi Arabia announced plans for a $5 billion green hydrogen project partly intended for the export of hydrogen in the form of ammonia to Japan.[53]

Hydrogen will probably become competitive for transport, especially heavy vehicles, aviation, and shipping, before it is competitive in providing power to back up variable renewables. The problem is that the overall efficiency of converting electric power into hydrogen and then back into electricity is only about 45%. Therefore, very cheap renewable power is needed. That should be available in the Middle East and other locations with plenty of sun or wind and space to install solar or wind generators. A country such as the UK, which is expected to rely heavily on wind energy, could use the surplus power available when wind conditions are at their best and demand is low. But this implies that the electrolysers will be used only part of the time, which increases the investment cost per kg of hydrogen produced. So imported hydrogen may eventually be more competitive.[54]

Many countries have now adopted national hydrogen strategies, and the EU has set itself the target of having 40 GW of electrolyser capacity by 2030. That is more than half of the UK's total generating capacity today.

The potential of hydrogen to play a major part in reducing CO_2 has been known for decades. Today, there has been very little progress. But there are ambitious plans for the future. This a key area where governments need to be bold and undertake major investments even though the outcome cannot be known with certainty.

Carbon Capture Use and Storage (CCUS)

A third of world CO_2 emissions in 2019 were from coal-fired power stations. Many of those stations are fairly new and 60% of them could still be operating in 2050. For instance, the average age of coal power stations in China, which generates more than half of the world's coal-powered electricity, is only 13 years, whereas the normal life of a station is at least 60 years.[55]

Perhaps all these stations will be retired early to achieve net zero by 2050, but it seems unlikely. The alternative is to capture the CO_2 emissions from these stations, as well as from remaining gas power stations, and to use them in chemical processes or store them in stable formations underground, a technology known as carbon capture use and storage (CCUS).

It is easy to imagine that to achieve net zero by 2050 we are going to have to capture and store, or find a use for, a lot of CO_2. Besides power generation, CCUS is needed to reduce emissions from industry and to produce low-carbon fuels for transport. And since not all emissions can be eliminated, we are going to have to compensate by extracting CO_2 from the air. Many experts believe that large-scale deployment of bioenergy with carbon capture and storage, known as BECCS, at present the most cost-effective option for "negative emissions", will be essential for net zero.

CCUS has two disadvantages. The most serious one is obvious. CCUS is an add-on to fossil power stations or other plants. Without carbon pricing of some kind, a plant with CCUS can never be competitive with one without. The exception is when a valuable use can be found for the CO_2. There are opportunities for this, for instance, to enhance production in oil fields or to manufacture synthetic fuels. But generally speaking, CCUS will only be viable with the benefit of government support, carbon pricing, or other regulation.

The other big disadvantage is that, with current technology, CCUS only removes up to 90% of the CO_2. Getting above that level becomes prohibitively expensive. So, a coal-fired power station with CCUS is still not entirely carbon-free.

CCUS has been a bit of a Cinderella among low-carbon technologies. It has attracted far less investment than renewables or nuclear power. Back in 2009, the IEA[56] set a target of developing 100 large-scale CCUS projects between 2010 and 2020, storing 300 million tonnes (Mt) of CO_2 a year. The outcome was a capacity of just 40Mt. There are some important new initiatives in Europe, the UK, and the US, but progress on CCUS remains far behind what is needed for net zero by 2050.

CCUS is beloved by politicians in coal-producing regions because it is almost the only green technology that can preserve mining jobs. However, in practice, warm words have not been followed through with support on the scale required to make a big difference.

CCUS has had a mixed reception from environmentalists. Compared to renewables, it is seen as "clunky", and an "end of pipe" solution that perpetuates the continuing reign of fossil fuels. Perhaps one day we will find more elegant technical solutions to the climate challenge. But time is desperately short and we will have to use the technologies that are available, including CCUS. The technology may be clunky, as they say, but there is a certain logic in putting carbon emissions back under the earth where they came from.

CCUS is in the frame at the 2023 Climate Summit to be held in the United Arab Emirates approaches. Sultan Al-Jaber, who will chair the summit is also the CEO of the Abu Dhabi National Oil Company. He has said that climate diplomacy should be "laser focused" on phasing out fossil fuel emissions while phasing up CCUS. In other words, reducing oil and gas production itself is not the prime objective. Christiana Figueres, the former Executive Secretary of the UNFCCC, has described this view as "dangerous" and "a direct threat to the survival of vulnerable nations" since "we do not have CCUS commercially available and viable over the next five to seven years".[57]

CCUS is one of the technologies that has been given a boost in the US by the wide range of subsidies for clean energy in President Biden's new Inflation Reduction Act, discussed further in the following. According to the Global CCS Institute, there are now 196 commercial facilities in the CCS project pipeline, capable of sequestering 244 M tonnes of CO_2 p.a. Even assuming that these all come to fruition, that isn't a very big dent in the 30 billion tonnes plus of CO_2 emitted in the world today, but it certainly suggests that there is momentum.

It isn't surprising that fossil fuel producers are looking for ways to carve out a role for oil and gas in a low-carbon world. If they are willing to put resources into developing CCS, that is all for the good. If it means that, under UAE chairmanship, the climate summit will row back on the options for reducing oil and gas demand, then Christiana Figueres is right to be concerned.

Other Options for Low-Carbon Electric Power

The above has covered the main options for generating electric power that are available on a significant scale today. Innumerable other possibilities have been proposed and are at various stages of research. But new technologies typically take a long time to reach the stage of mass deployment where they can have a significant impact on world energy. 2050 is only 27 years away. Solar power was already in use for satellites in the 1960s and was starting to be deployed in the US in the early 1980s. More than 40 years later, it is only now beginning to realise its full potential. Wind energy started to be commercialised in the late 1970s.

This makes it fairly unlikely, though of course not impossible, that a new technology will make a really significant contribution towards global low-carbon electricity by 2050.

One notable contender is nuclear fusion. It would be a wonderful thing if we could capture the energy of the sun by combining small atoms at very high temperatures. Research has been conducted on a large scale since the 1970s. By 2023, the record for sustained fusion is five seconds.

The current flagship of nuclear fusion is a huge international project located in France called ITER based on magnetic confinement technology. The EU, the UK, Russia, Japan, China, and the US are all participants. In some ways, it is a model for global cooperation in technology. But, not surprisingly, it has been plagued by internal politics. If it is successful in generating sustained fusion, and if governments are prepared to continue with large-scale funding, it could lead to the construction of a demonstration fusion power station in the 2030s. On that pathway, nuclear fusion will be too late to contribute much to net zero in 2050.

There are other projects, generally on a smaller scale, using different fusion technologies, some of which aim to produce useful fusion power much sooner. In December 2022, the US Lawrence Livermore National Laboratory announced that, for the first time, a fusion experiment had generated net positive energy. This uses alternative laser technology. It is a "one shot every two weeks type machine" that is a long way from being a useful power generator.[58]

The UK government is promoting another fusion project that is still at the design stage: the Spherical Tokamak for Energy Production. Like ITER, this uses magnetic confinement technology. While the talk is positive, it remains to be seen whether the government, or commercial backers, will support it right through to the construction stage, when the costs will run into billions.

According to the Fusion Industry Association, 33 private fusion companies have raised a total of $4.9 billion of funding, including $117 million of government grants.[59] Nobody spends this kind of money on a fantasy.

A real breakthrough in fusion technology would certainly be significant. Perhaps nuclear fusion will eventually provide the abundant, reliable, affordable, low-cost energy with minimal environmental impact that will save the planet. But it has been a long time coming. It's the Holy Grail of energy technologies, but the knights are still questing in the wasteland.

The various forms of marine energy, from waves, tides, or tidal barrages, have been tested over many decades, especially in the UK which seems like an ideal location. But success has been limited. These are examples of several technologies where really large-scale investment over a period of years might yield reliable, competitive low-carbon energy, but governments or other investors would have to take a big risk.

Buildings Heating and Cooling

Cooling

The demand for air conditioning is growing rapidly around the world as a result of increasing affluence and rising temperatures. Two-thirds of the market today is in China, the US, and Japan, but it is in India and Indonesia that demand is growing most rapidly, at around 10% p.a. since 2010. Energy consumption has more than tripled since 1990 and air conditioning now consumes about 7% of world electricity generation. As long as electric power is based on fossil fuels, there is a vicious cycle as rising temperatures promote the demand for more air conditioning.

According to the IEA, most new air conditioning units are two or three times less efficient than the best available models, so there is potential for large savings through tighter government regulation.[60]

Air conditioning is a good fit with photovoltaic generation. Maximum demand is when the sun is at its hottest. Admittedly the demand for cooling may continue after the sun has set but electric batteries are now well adapted for managing a gap of a few hours between supply and demand. High demand for air conditioning during a series of overcast days will pose more of a problem.

Heating

Half of the world's energy supply is used for heating. That includes industrial heat, which is discussed separately in the following. Space heating in homes and service buildings accounts for about 8% of global CO_2 emissions. Gas is the most common source of space heating today, with coal, gas, and electricity all having significant roles. Coal is especially used in China. With growing affluence, the world's heated residential floor area increased by 20% between 2010 and 2020 but energy demand increased by only 10%, reflecting a shift from coal, oil, and gas towards renewables, improvements in the efficiency of boilers, and better insulation of buildings.[61]

The main technologies needed to reduce CO_2 emissions from buildings are efficient building design and insulation, and the substitution of electric heat pumps or hydrogen for fossil fuels.

Heat pumps concentrate the heat in the air or the ground thus multiplying the heat delivered by electric power. That is based on Gay-Lussac's physical law, "As the pressure of a particular mass of gas goes up the temperature also goes up, and vice versa". In a closed system, the gas takes on the temperature of the air or the ground. It is then pressurised so that the temperature increases and is then passed through a heat exchanger to heat water for radiators or under pipes. The gas is then de-pressurised and returns to the air or ground system. It's the exact reverse of the operation of a refrigerator.

An air source heat pump can achieve a multiple of around three of the heat that the electric power itself could generate, though this may decline in cold weather, and a ground source heat pump a multiple of four. This makes heating with electricity much more affordable. Heat pumps do not have anything like the power and flexibility of a gas boiler. The hot water that they produce is of relatively low temperature and this means that buildings have to be well insulated and radiators have to be larger. This is easier to achieve with new, purpose-designed, buildings than with existing housing stock.

This is one of the most significant areas that will test the public's willingness to put up with a degree of additional cost and inconvenience in the interest of the climate challenge.

The UK government has announced that new gas boilers will be banned for new houses from 2025 and altogether from 2035. It has also announced significant grants to help with the cost of alternatives. This will involve considerable cost and political nerve. It is to be hoped that the government sticks to its guns. Similar proposals in Germany are so hotly contested that they risk breaking up the coalition government.

The alternative low-carbon heating option for buildings is hydrogen. Hydrogen could be blended into, and eventually replace, existing gas supply. It can be burnt in gas boilers with limited modification. Blue hydrogen would be the most affordable option but it is unpopular with environmentalists because it involves continuing gas production and CCUS. Green hydrogen would be fully carbon-free but it looks expensive at the moment.

Hydrogen would be a better substitute for gas than heat pumps in terms of heating power. It would be less disruptive for existing homes. However, it is a big drawback that hydrogen can only be introduced as part of a local or regional system. A government or a major supply company has to finance and manage the conversion of the local grid to hydrogen. A certain proportion of hydrogen can be introduced without changing the burning appliances. But for full conversion, significant changes are needed. Everyone has to shift at once. The feasibility of making the switch needs to be tested. The UK government's plans to conduct such a test, in a village in Cheshire, had to be abandoned in July 2023 when residents objected.

Heat pumps on the other hand can be introduced gradually, house by house. Mainly for this reason, it seems likely that heat pumps will be the most widely adopted solution for the heating of buildings.

Industry

After electricity generation, industry is the biggest source of CO_2 emissions, contributing about a quarter of the world's total. More than 70% of these emissions are from iron and steel production, chemicals, and cement. As in so many other areas, China is by far the biggest player. About half the world's cement, iron, and steel are made in China.

These products are needed on a vast scale for economic development, for roads, railways, and buildings of all kinds. They are also needed for low-carbon transition because wind generation, nuclear power, and CCUS all require large amounts of concrete and steel.

Decarbonisation of heavy industry presents a particular challenge because it is difficult for electricity to achieve the very high temperatures required and because coal or gas contribute not only heat but also necessary chemical inputs. The process of manufacturing cement is inherently carbon-emitting.

Substantial gains are possible through electrification where possible and improvements in efficiency. Changes in the cement-making process and its ingredients can significantly reduce emissions. Winning the confidence of the construction industry, often conservative in outlook, for changes in the make-up of cement is a particular challenge. About a third of steel production is from scrap and this is already made with electric arc furnaces. There is also huge potential for redesigning vehicles and buildings to reduce the need for new steel and concrete.

However, reaching net zero will require fundamental changes to the way in which steel is produced and the unavoidable emissions from cement-making will need to be captured and stored. Hydrogen can contribute both the heat and the chemical input needed for steelmaking. Bioenergy could also contribute, but heavy industry will probably lag behind other sectors.

High temperature nuclear reactors, discussed above, are also a possible source of high-level heat for industry.

Steel and chemicals, especially, are traded around the world in competitive markets, and this means that any country imposing low-carbon obligations will have to either compensate its domestic industry or impose some kind of carbon charge on imports. It is not surprising that pressure for such charges is growing, especially in Europe and the US. The "Carbon Border Adjustment Mechanisms" being proposed by the EU and the US are discussed in Chapter 4.

The EU has launched a $157 million project to demonstrate steelmaking from hydrogen on a commercial scale. The aim is for around 30% of EU primary steel-making to be decarbonised by 2030 using hydrogen derived from renewables. The costs are uncertain and this is likely to require substantial government support in the form of regulation and or carbon incentives. The European Clean Steel Partnership estimates that €2.6 billion will need to be spent on R&D by 2030.

The first EU-funded large-scale CCUS project for cement-making is expected to come into operation in 2027.[62] The European cement industry is also gearing up to reduce emissions by 30% by 2030.[63]

In 2019, China's second largest steelmaker, HBIS Group, announced plans to build a full scale steel plant using hydrogen.

According to research by Bloomberg, steel from hydrogen could become competitive with steel made using coking coal by 2030. By 2050, world steel-making could become carbon-free using a combination of recycling and hydrogen. But $278 billion of investment is needed to bring this about.[64]

This is typical of the dilemmas that governments face in their net zero plans. The technology is known but it hasn't yet been applied on a commercial scale. Initial costs of creating the necessary infrastructure are substantial. Widespread application should bring costs down, perhaps quite dramatically, but it is difficult to judge how fast and how soon. What is clear is that major investment is required. However, according to the World Steel Association, the energy costs of the hydrogen-based technology would be more than five times the costs of traditional coal-based technology: "Hydrogen production levels and its costs will therefore need to be resolved for it to become a viable solution. This will require engagement and funding".[65]

The first nations in the field will have to bear the costs but may also win new export industries. On the other hand, as happened after Germany invested heavily in solar photovoltaics at a time when costs were still high, manufacturing may quickly shift to lower cost regions.

Transport

Transport is the fastest growing emissions sector. 21% of global CO_2 emissions are derived from transport. That includes 8% from cars, 4% from heavy-duty trucks, 2% from aviation, and 2% from shipping. Rail, buses, and industrial vehicles make up the rest.

Cars and Light Vehicles

There have been big gains in the efficiency of conventional petrol and diesel vehicles. But to achieve net zero, alternative technologies will be needed. At present, electrification seems by far the most promising option for light vehicles, although low-carbon fuels and hydrogen are significant possible alternatives, especially for heavier vehicles.

The progress of electric vehicles powered by lithium-ion batteries is a model of low-carbon technical progress. The worlds of technology, business, finance, and government have come together to deliver change at a super-charged pace.

The price of electric batteries declined by 90% between 2010 and 2021 thanks partly to technical progress but mainly volume production.[66] Sales of electric vehicles have rocketed from 125,000 in 2012 to 6.7 m in 2021, when they represented 8% of world light vehicle sales. In China, sales were 3.3 m, in Europe, 2.3 m, and in North America, 0.7 m.[67] In the UK, sales of electric vehicles, including plug-in hybrids, rose by more than 70% in 2021 to reach 18% of all sales. If one includes hybrids of all kinds, the figure is 45%.[68]

The phenomenon of Tesla illustrates just how dynamic the business world can be. Tesla captured the public's imagination with the first up-market electric vehicles. Its sales rose from a few thousand in 2013 to nearly 500,000 in 2021 and the company is projecting sales growth of around 50% p.a. for the future. Tesla has been loss-making for most of its life and is only marginally profitable today. But the financial markets love it because they think it represents the future. At its peak, the market valued Tesla at more than ten times the value of VW or Mercedes-Benz and more than five times the value of Toyota, which was the next most highly valued company.

Governments have piled in with their support. In the US, there is a tax credit of $7,500 for buying an electric car. Most countries in Europe have similar incentives, for example, Germany which offers €3,000. The UK is phasing out its subsidies, as sales of electric cars have increased dramatically, and is concentrating its support on strengthening the charging network. China also is phasing out its subsidies and is instead imposing mandates on the manufacturers.

All this has had a dramatic effect on the industry. The manufacturers have got the message and they are rapidly increasing the share of electric vehicles in their ranges. According to Reuters, the world industry plans to invest more than £500 billion in electric vehicles and batteries by 2030.

Impressive as these developments are, they do not imply that all is plain sailing for the decarbonisation of light vehicles. Electric vehicles still have a long way to go in terms of market share. Now that the networks of charging points are growing and new vehicles commonly have a range in excess of 200 miles, motorists' "range anxiety" is probably receding. But electric vehicles are still more expensive than conventional vehicles, mainly due to the cost of batteries. Battery costs have been coming down and may continue to do so, but the cost of materials such as lithium, cobalt, and nickel has been increasing and this may slow or even reverse this process for a year or two.

There is potential for further technical advances, especially through solid-state batteries, but opinion is divided on how soon these might become available.

Electric cars by themselves do not ensure a low-carbon outcome. That depends on their being supplied with low-carbon electricity and on low-carbon vehicle manufacturing, both of which are a long way off in many parts of the world. Electric cars are also heavier than conventional vehicles and cause more wear and tear on the roads.

The main alternatives for light vehicles are hydrogen fuel cells or low-carbon fuels. Hydrogen fuel cells are a proven option, but there are only about 25,000 examples in the world today. In contrast to electric vehicles, they suffer from the lack of existing infrastructure. Someone would have to make a huge investment in hydrogen supply and recharging for them to become attractive to ordinary motorists. They may be more suitable for service vehicles with fixed routes that can be recharged at the base.

There is a wide range of options for low-carbon vehicle fuels. Most European countries have obligations for the blending of ethanol from bio sources in petrol and diesel, and in Brazil, ethanol derived from sugar cane residues contributes 20–25% of fuel for cars. Little or no modification of internal combustion engines is required. However, in Europe, these obligations are running into difficulty as the EU Commission tightens its rules on sustainability. Palm oil no longer counts towards the quotas because of concern that it encourages deforestation. There are concerns that other sources of feedstock are displacing food production. Not surprisingly, producer countries are not too happy with the growing restrictions and, for instance, Indonesia is challenging the exclusion of palm oil at the World Trade Organization. Ethanol will probably continue to play some role in the decarbonisation of vehicles, but the potential for growth is clouded by the limitations on feedstock supply from genuinely sustainable sources.

Methanol derived from green hydrogen, discussed above, is another possible option for low-carbon propulsion that does not require major engine modification. But it is expensive today. Nobody is going down that route on a large scale at present.

China, the EU, and the State of California are proposing bans on the sale of new petrol or diesel cars from 2035 and the UK from 2030. However, there are plenty of examples of governments backing down on future environmental commitments, and as the time for implementation draws near, the costs become apparent, and industry lobbying becomes more frantic. For instance, a commitment by the UK government that by 2016 all new houses would be zero carbon was withdrawn in 2015 for exactly these reasons.[69] Today, the EU Commission is struggling to maintain its aim of phasing out internal combustion engines against vigorous lobbying by the German and Italian motor industries.

It is to be hoped that governments will hold their nerve to end the sale of new conventional cars, although recent backtracking by the UK government is worrying. As already mentioned, the industry is investing heavily in the transition, and the sale of electric vehicles is growing rapidly, especially in the developed world and China.

Converting the developing world to electric vehicles will, similarly, depend on the development of charging infrastructure.

Further technical progress to reduce the weight and increase the range of electric vehicles can be expected. Government and industry need to work together to vastly increase the availability of charging points. Costs may also come down and some are predicting that the price of electric vehicles may reach parity with conventional vehicles by 2030.[70]

A huge increase in lithium supply will be needed for the electrification of light vehicles using current technology. It is hard to judge whether this could be a problem. Lithium deposits are widely spread across the globe, and there is lithium in sea water. Most of today's supply has been extracted from rocks. Australia and Chile are the main mining countries, but more than half the ore processing takes place in China. The price of lithium has fluctuated wildly as production rates struggle to meet demand. It is certainly possible that rising lithium prices will slow or even for a time reverse the reduction in the cost of electric vehicles that can otherwise be expected due to technical progress and mass production. In the longer term, recycling of lithium from retired batteries will make an increasing contribution.[71]

Alternative battery technologies that use sodium in place of lithium are under development, but, in the view of the International Renewable Energy Agency (IRENA), "lithium will remain the material of choice for the foreseeable future".

There will also need to be an increase in the supply of certain rare earths needed for permanent magnets.[72] The amounts required are much smaller than for lithium and there are ample deposits available around the world. They occur as trace elements in rocks that are often radioactive. Mining and processing them is costly and hazardous. Nearly 60% of the mining, and 90% of the processing, of rare earths takes place in China as well as 90% of permanent magnet production. So, China has a near monopoly on a resource that is needed not only for electric vehicles but also for wind generators and advanced weapons. This monopoly could certainly be broken, but it would take time to build up alternative industries. China has in the past threatened to withhold supplies as a lever in trade talks, but has never actually done so.[73] It might not be in China's long-term interests, but it could certainly cause serious pain to the West for a while. So the state of relations between China and the West could have an impact on the progress of electric vehicles at least for a period.

Heavy Vehicles

Light trucks and vans, and to some extent medium-weight trucks, fall into the same category as light vehicles. They are suitable for electrification, and a wide range of new models is now being produced.

Buses and goods vehicles with fixed routes are particularly suitable for electrification because they can be recharged, or have their batteries replaced, at their depot or even at one or two stations en route.

However, heavy goods vehicles (HGVs) driving long and changing routes pose a particular problem. Batteries with sufficient capacity are expensive and heavy, and this inevitably eats into the potential payload. Charging with current technology may cause significant delay. Electrified heavy-duty trucks exist, but there are only about 66,000 of them on the roads today, representing 0.1% of worldwide stock.

Possibly with improvements in batteries and recharging facilities, electrified HGVs will become the norm. There is a debate in the industry about this. Electrification of main roads, through overhead wires or sub-surface induction coils, could greatly reduce the battery ranges required. But these would be major investments.

The likely alternatives are biofuels or hydrogen-powered fuel cells. The range of possible biofuels includes biodiesel, biomethane, or "lignocellulosic" fuels drawn from woody plant materials. Like other biofuel uses, these depend on the availability of sustainable bio materials and the priorities to be given for their use. As described above, methanol produced from green hydrogen is another low-carbon fuel that may become competitive if governments adopt hydrogen-intensive strategies.

HGVs will lag behind lighter vehicles and, depending to some extent on timing, the costs of decarbonisation are likely to be higher. But, as governments progressively tighten the screw on vehicle emissions, the necessary low-carbon technologies for HGVs are available.

Aviation

Aviation contributes about 2% of global CO_2 emissions. This may seem a modest share but it is more than some major economies, such as the UK, contribute and it is growing rapidly. It is also one of the most difficult sources to control and reduce.

More and more people want to fly. Between 2000 and 2015, passenger demand grew at an average of 5% p.a. Because of improvements in aircraft design and the efficiency of aeroengines, the growth in emissions was significantly less, at 2.3%, but that is still rapid growth. The COVID-19 pandemic caused demand and emissions to fall sharply in 2020 and 2021, but they have been recovering rapidly since then.

There are three main options for reducing and eventually eliminating aircraft CO_2 emissions. These are electrification, hydrogen, and sustainable fuels.

Electric flying "taxis" are already being introduced. However, with present technology, the weight of batteries severely restricts both the size and range of battery electric planes. Hydrogen can power jet engines or can generate electricity through fuels cells. The issues here are the cost and availability of green hydrogen and the storage of hydrogen under pressure in the aircraft.

Sustainable fuels can be made from plant materials or they can be synthetic. Aviation may, therefore, be one of the uses that will have to compete for the limited supply of genuinely sustainable feedstock. The affordability of synthetic fuels will depend on the cost and availability of green hydrogen and, ironically, CO_2.

In 2016, the International Civil Aviation Organization (ICAO), which is the UN agency for air travel, reached an agreement to cap future emissions at 2020 levels or purchase offsetting credits. Most governments have signed up to this, but Russia and India declined on the grounds that it imposed an unfair burden on emerging countries.[74]

More recently, in 2021, the International Air Transport Association (IATA), which represents world airlines, committed the industry to achieving net-zero emissions by 2050. Their plan is to achieve this 65% through sustainable fuel, 13% through hydrogen or electrification, 3% through efficiency improvements, 11% through CCS in fuel manufacture, and 8% through offsets. They expect that electric and hydrogen aircraft for the regional market will become available by 2035.

All the options for major reductions in aviation emissions, except perhaps gains in efficiency, appear costly with current technology. As IATA said in their announcement, "Governments must be active partners. The costs and investment risks are too high otherwise. Limiting flying with … taxes would stifle investment and could limit flying to the wealthy". This is the dilemma in a nutshell. The public who have access to cheap flights and those in developing countries who aspire to air travel are not going to give this up easily. To achieve net zero in aviation governments will have to make some major investments.

Shipping

At 2% of the global total, CO_2 emissions from shipping are in the same range as aviation. They also have been growing, although not as rapidly. They rose by 9% in the ten years to 2018. They fell sharply in 2019 and 2020, due to COVID-19 but have been recovering since.[75]

Larger vessels and improved hull designs have already reduced the carbon intensity of shipping significantly. Other efficiency measures could include slower steaming and the provision of low-carbon electric power while ships are in harbour.

Getting shipping emission levels down to really low levels will require alternative fuels. Electric batteries may be suitable for smaller vessels on short runs. But the low power density by weight makes them unsuitable for large ocean-going ships.

Other options are similar to those for vehicles. Hydrogen has low energy intensity by volume and has to be stored under pressure or liquefied at very low temperatures. These problems can be addressed by converting hydrogen to methanol or ammonia. The underlying problem is the need to find an affordable source of green hydrogen. At present these look like expensive options.

Plant-based fuels such as ethanol are probably the most suitable for marine use and do not require major modifications of existing engines. As with other potential uses of ethanol, the problem is the limited supply of genuinely sustainable feedstock.

The International Maritime Organization (IMO) of the UN set out its "initial strategy" for emissions reduction from shipping in 2018. This calls for a 40% reduction of emissions intensity by 2030 and a 50% reduction in total emissions by 2050. The strategy focuses on efficiency measures in the short term but recognises that alternative fuels or energy sources will be essential in the medium and longer term. A revised strategy, announced in July 2023, sets an "enhanced common ambition to reach net-zero greenhouse gas emissions close to 2050".[76] However, there is not much detail on how this is to be achieved and the IMO recognises that the strategy is "a starting point for the work that needs to intensify".

The transport of coal, oil, gas, and derivative products accounts for 40% of all shipping by weight. So, there should be significantly less need for shipping in a net zero world.

Geoengineering

The last resort of technical options is geoengineering, interfering with the atmosphere to counter-act global warming. This is rightly viewed with great suspicion because it is hard to know what the ultimate consequences might be and because of fears that geoengineering might provide an excuse to let up on the effort to reduce emissions. These are not attractive options but they should continue to be the subject of research. The topic of geoengineering is discussed further in a postscript to this book.

Conclusion

It seems clear that our best hope lies in an electric future. The progress of renewables has made low-carbon electricity affordable. Demand for electricity is already expanding rapidly around the world. Some of the fastest growing sectors, such as air conditioning, IT, communications, and much of the high value-added industry, are already electric. And it now appears that electricity is the likely low-carbon medium for most vehicles and for the heating of buildings. Electricity can also play a part, although probably a limited one, in heavy industry, aviation, and shipping.

So, the first priority should be those technologies that complement this electric revolution. First among these are electric batteries. There are options that may have the potential to greatly improve their performance and reduce costs. Governments should work with industry to bring that forward. Hydrogen generated by electrolysis is also a complement to renewable electricity because, in various chemical forms, it enables power to be stored, delivered in vehicles, and shipped internationally on a large scale. Hydrogen may also be an option for heavy industry and for aviation. So working to reduce the cost of hydrogen production by electrolysis should also be a top priority. Heat pumps can bring down the cost of electric power for domestic heating.

Nuclear power can provide low-carbon base load power. It may not be ideal as a back-up for renewables but, leaving aside hydropower, it is by far the largest source of reliable low-carbon power that we have today and there are interesting possibilities for smaller and more advanced reactor designs.

Carbon capture and storage may well be needed eventually to achieve negative emissions and to deal with some of the most difficult challenges facing heavy industry. Advanced biofuels may be needed for low-carbon aviation.

All these technologies are likely to be needed in a net zero world. Some of them require further technical development, but almost all of them require major investment to achieve mass deployment and start to drive down the cost. Governments must be prepared to invest heavily to get them over this hurdle, after which regulation and commercial forces can be expected to continue the process of deployment. That is Key Policy No. 2. It is not risk-free. The potential for cost reductions is hard to predict and, to varying degrees, these technologies will compete with each other in various applications. There will be losers as well as winners. But governments will have to be prepared to invest heavily and take some well-considered risks. That is the second key policy to save the planet.

Governments also need programmes of blue sky research, which industry will certainly not deliver, and some engagement in "wild card" options that are far from being commercial today, such as nuclear fusion, microbial energy, ocean energy, and geothermal energy. Not everyone has to invest in these options, but hopefully, at least one major nation will explore the potential of each of them.

Ideally, governments would cooperate to divide up the load, share results, and avoid duplication. The potential for that is limited in the competitive world that we live in. Governments are much too concerned about falling behind to leave any of the major technologies entirely to others and may be unwilling to share near-commercial information. These tendencies are exacerbated by global political tensions. Indeed, today, international competition and the fear of falling behind are motivating major new investment programmes in the US and probably also in Europe. There are promising signs, but there is much more to be done.

Chapter 3

Business and Public Opinion: Creating a Deep Appetite for Change

Key Policy No. 3.

Business is the activator, but to achieve the scale and pace of change required, it needs strong government policies to shift the economic playing field in favour of low-carbon technology. Governments can only act with the support of public opinion and this gives those who can influence opinion a critical role. Persuading the public to adapt is Key Policy No. 3. We have to create a deep appetite for change. Too often influencers have avoided the challenge.

Business

The role of business, including the financial community, is central. Business will have to deploy the low-carbon technologies that are required, the financial community will have to find the money, and business will have a big part in persuading consumers to adopt low-carbon alternatives. Business is creative. It has immense capacity for innovation and for learning from experience and these will be drivers of low-carbon transformation.

There are plenty of signs that business has begun to take climate change seriously. The Glasgow Summit saw a step change in business involvement. "I've seen more CEOs here in the last eight days than I have in the previous eight years of *Climate Summits*", one senior figure was reported as saying.[77]

We have seen a big change, in recent years, in the attitude of business. Companies are acknowledging their responsibilities, reporting on their environmental and climate impacts, and setting themselves ambitious, mostly long-term, targets. Finance companies and rating agencies are supporting this trend.

In recent years, there has been a significant increase in business investment in clean energy, including renewables and efficiency, and some decline in upstream oil and gas development.[78] The share of clean energy and energy efficiency in total energy investment rose from 31% in 2017 to 42% in 2021. The impact was enhanced by the fact that the cost of a unit of wind and solar output has declined more than four fold since 2010. You get a lot more bang for your buck. But so far the increase in spending on low-carbon energy is nothing like what is required. According to the IEA, spending would need to double by 2030 to put us on course for 2°C and it would need to triple for 1.5°C. A particular weakness is that Emerging Markets and Developing Economies (EMDEs), which represent two-thirds of the global population, account for only one-fifth of global investment in clean energy, showing that business is still a long way from meeting the critical need for low-carbon infrastructure in the developing world.

Businesspeople have vision and they understand, increasingly, that the future prospects of their organisations depend on adapting successfully to a low-carbon world. Indeed, ideally, on leading the low-carbon transformation. But business has to be practical. In order to survive, companies have to make profits today or at least to present credible pathways to making profits. Shareholders and financiers, including green financiers, expect a good return. Green funds recruit investors on the basis that they will be more profitable than investments in fossil fuel-based sectors. They do not, for the most part, invite selfless investors to lose money in a good cause.

We can see the dilemma that business faces in the recent announcements of BlackRock, the biggest investment fund of all. BlackRock believes that "climate risk is investment risk and ... climate risk and the energy transition are already transforming both the real economy and how people invest in it". But BlackRock also announced that in 2022 it expected to support fewer climate-related shareholder proposals than in 2021. "BlackRock notes that many of the climate-related shareholder proposals coming to a vote in 2022 are more prescriptive ... and may not promote long-time shareholder value".[79] In other words, providing information is fine, but trying to force companies to go down low-carbon avenues that their management don't think are sufficiently profitable is not.

The main constraint on the ability of business to deliver is not the availability of funds. The funds available for investment across the world are so vast that they can be regarded as limitless as far as the climate transformation is concerned. The Glasgow Financial Alliance for Net Zero, set up at the Glasgow Summit as the name suggests, is supported by finance companies with $130 trillion of private capital. Much more critical is the availability of profitable investment opportunities with acceptable risk. Where these are available, the money will flow.

There is a lot that business can do on its own initiative in terms of improving efficiency, minimising packaging and promoting recycling, designing less carbon-intensive products, and increasing relevant R&D. In some countries, wind and solar power with complementary batteries are now so competitive that government subsidies are not needed.

But for the next big changes in technology, to address difficult areas such as heavy industry, heating, transport, aviation, and shipping, industry will depend on governments to create the necessary conditions through taxation, regulation, or other positive support. The impact of greenhouse gas emissions on the environment is an "externality". Emissions reductions do not automatically come through to the bottom line unless government acts to put a price on carbon, subsidise low-carbon options, or otherwise regulate to tilt the playing field. To get to net zero by 2050 requires a very rapid pace of change. Probably, without government intervention low-carbon electricity will gradually achieve an ascendancy over fossil fuels, but not fast enough for net zero.

Green funds and pro climate business policies, such as those based around "Environmental, Social, and Governance" (ESG) analysis, can make industry more responsive to green investment opportunities. BlackRock may have been cautious about "prescriptive" shareholder interventions, but they were much more positive on shareholder proposals seeking better information. "We look to company leadership to disclose to investors how climate risks and opportunities might impact their business and how these factors are addressed".

There have also been rapid developments in financial reporting since the Financial Stability Board of the G20 set up its Task Force on Climate-Related Financial Disclosures (TCFD) in 2015. This body's framework for reporting climate risks and opportunities and how they are managed has gained increasing traction. Companies with $194 trillion of assets now support this initiative. A survey by the TCFD found a rapid increase in disclosure in 2020, with 52% of companies surveyed reporting climate risks and opportunities and 44% "climate-related metrics".[80]

It has now become a standard requirement for large businesses, at least in the West, to cover ESG in their annual reports. "Environmental" is taken to include climate change, carbon emissions, pollution, and waste management among other topics. According to the major US investment research company Morningstar, about $2.6 trillion of assets are now managed in more than 2,900 ESG funds.[81]

A number of governments, notably the EU, Japan, and the UK, are moving to make climate disclosure in company reports mandatory. The International Financial Reporting Standards Foundation (IFRSF) is clarifying the requirements for the reporting of sustainability in company accounts, and the credit rating agencies are increasingly taking sustainability issues into account in their reports.

The growth of green finance is a part of this. According to the Climate Bonds Initiative, the global issue of green bonds has been growing rapidly in recent years reaching about $300 billion in 2020, of which $120 billion was private sector ($55 billion finance corporate and $65 billion non-finance corporate). The biggest issuers were the US, China, and France. Public sector issuance has been rising faster than private sector issuance. But only $46 billion of the total was in emerging economies.

There is no single definition of what counts as a green bond, although a number of influential standards have been issued.[82] It is difficult to judge the "additionality" of green bonds, in other words, whether they make possible green projects that could not otherwise have been financed. The rates of return and security requirements are not greatly different from ordinary bonds. In some cases, they may simply free up funds for investment in other "dirty" projects of the same business. However, they do require issuing companies to pay attention and account for the environmental impact of at least some of their investments and they provide better access to environmental investment funds.

It is difficult to measure a company's performance on climate change objectively. Some 100 organisations offer ESG ratings, and this number has doubled in a year.[83] However, according to a study by MIT Sloan School of Management and the University of Zurich, the ratings of different providers "disagree substantially".[84]

The difficulty is illustrated by the 2022 report of the shareholder advocacy group As You Sow. The report ranked major corporations on their contributions to reducing greenhouse gas emissions. There were three criteria: disclosure, targets, and reductions. Microsoft came top and Tesla bottom. Surely an odd result since Tesla has, arguably, done more than any other company to promote the cause of emissions reduction. No doubt Microsoft's reporting and internal emissions control were judged excellent and Tesla's as relatively poor.

There are important aspects of green performance that can be assessed in a fairly straightforward way. How energy efficient are a company's offices, or processes that lend themselves to comparison? Do organisations at least have management structures and information systems that enable them to assess, and take into account, the environmental implications of their business decisions? These things all matter. They cover basic housekeeping. They are significant for reducing carbon emissions, but, as the Tesla rating demonstrates, they are not the whole story. It is far more difficult to measure objectively the full impact of a business on climate change.

Some companies are in sectors, such as most services, which don't have major emissions. They can insulate their offices, buy a heat pump, put PV on the roof, cut down on executive travel, and plant trees. It's important and it all contributes, but it isn't the biggest deal. They may also be providing services that are critical to the transformation of sectors of the economy that are big emitters, but that is more difficult to judge and evaluate.

The companies that are the biggest emitters today, working in areas such as oil and gas, iron and steel, chemicals, cement, and motor manufacturing, may also be among the companies that will play the biggest parts in achieving the energy transition. Even "good" companies that are investing in wind or solar power need further evaluation. Building a wind farm to meet government requirements in a developed country is certainly a worthwhile green project. But the businesses and financial organisations that are really changing the course of global decarbonisation are the ones that are carving out and delivering pioneering green projects, including in the developing world.

For a government, net zero is a meaningful target, even if far into the future. For a company, it may be less significant, because companies can choose which lines of business they are in. Nothing is easier than to sell off a carbon-producing activity to another organisation, perhaps unquoted, that is less concerned about its environmental image. Company emissions are reduced, but the benefit to the environment is zero, or perhaps negative.

There is no metric or set of metrics that enable investors to judge the overall climate performance of individual businesses. We should be deeply suspicious of "black box" assessments that claim to do this without revealing the inner workings. One has to look at each company within the context of its business sector and the options available to promote or retard the low-carbon transition. Investors also have to consider how their behaviour is most likely to influence the company one way or the other.

It is certainly desirable to standardise the process of ESG assessment as much as possible. The World Economic Forum is one of the organisations that is trying to achieve this.[85] But in the end, investors will have to turn to experts in the field with knowledge of specific industries whom they trust. In many cases, active engagement to understand and influence company policy may lead to a better outcome for the environment than bailing out based on limited analysis. This is labour intensive and only possible, directly, between major investment houses and major businesses. Others will have to rely on the recommendation of agencies of one kind or another. But their advice should be based on demonstrated knowledge of specific industries and published reasoning.

The IEA makes projections of future oil and gas demand in its 2022 World Energy Outlook. In its net zero case, oil demand falls by a quarter to 2030 and by two-thirds to 2040. In their Stated Policies case, oil demand continues to increase to 2050. In Announced Pledges, there is no reduction to 2030, but demand falls by just over 50% to 2050. Gas demand is somewhat more persistent. So, we can expect the world to be significantly dependent on oil and gas for several decades to come. Hopefully, we will be closer to the net zero outcome, but that, unfortunately, is not guaranteed. All this suggests that we are in for a bumpy ride on oil and perhaps gas prices. Future demand is hard to predict and OPEC has no interest in over producing. Even if prices are due to decline in the longer term, we can expect some serious price spikes along the way.

Big Oil

The Stone Age didn't end because they ran out of stones. People discovered and adopted superior materials, notably bronze and eventually iron. The same is true of the oil and gas age. Oil and gas production will decline when motorists and industry improve their efficiency and switch to more advanced low-carbon sources of energy faster than the growth in their demand for energy services, and not before. Producers in the Middle East, Africa, Russia, and South America, who control the vast majority of reserves and dominate oil production, will produce to meet demand. If they didn't, Western governments would scramble to increase their own production, because security of supply will always trump the environment. The vital services of society including health, sanitation, education, and security all depend on people being able to get around by car. Other uses may be less essential, but who is willing to introduce petrol controls that restrict the mobility of ordinary citizens? We are looking for a transition, not a train crash.

The oil and gas industries are not free from criticism. There may well be other legitimate environmental or social reasons for challenging some of their investments. But as a means of limiting climate change, beating on the oil companies to reduce production is almost entirely fruitless. Some may argue that high-profile campaigns nevertheless raise awareness of the climate challenge. Perhaps so. But this is really displacement activity which encourages the public to put the climate crisis down to the misdeeds of distant decision makers in industry and government when, in fact, it is our own consumption that is at the root of the problem. It is true that consumers have limited ability to change their sources of energy unless government and industry act to create the necessary opportunities. But equally, government and industry cannot drive radical change until consumers are willing to adapt and to bear the cost.

We see this most clearly in the reaction to the loss of oil and gas supply that has been caused by the war in Ukraine. Oil and gas prices have risen sharply and there have been concerns about shortages. Europe has achieved a substantial reduction in gas demand. But at the same time, driven by public opinion, governments have made energetic efforts to increase the supply of fossil fuels. The UK has accelerated licensing to increase oil production in the North Sea. Europe has rapidly installed new facilities to import liquefied natural gas. Coal plants have reopened and closures have been put on hold. Fossil fuel supplies have been subsidised.

This is not an irrational response because high energy prices cause real hardship to the less well-off who cannot avoid spending on energy, for instance, to keep warm or travel to work. The hardship is at its worst in developing countries for whom energy import costs are a major burden and where non-fossil options, such as electrified public transport, are least developed. For so long as the world's infrastructure for transport, heating, industry, and electricity generation remains largely based on fossil fuels, consumers and governments will not be able to endure shortages of oil, gas, or even coal.

A look at the web sites of major environmental NGOs still shows a preoccupation with campaigns against oil and gas companies and limited recognition that hard choices will be required and that the general public will have to adapt. Greenpeace UK is perhaps the most egregious. "The government isn't rising to the … challenge … the solutions cost less than those dirty technologies straight off the shelf. It should be a no-brainer … the fossil fuel industry is blocking progress".[86] Friends of the Earth International blame "the concentration of power over energy goods and services in the hands of the few".[87] The article that leads on the Sierra Club's climate site describes an IPCC report and then goes straight into an attack on EXXON Mobil.[88] The World Wildlife Fund

(WWF)'s site is significantly better, however, "We must rethink the way we produce and consume energy, food, and water ... and help people prepare for a changing world ... achieving this future will require action by everyone".[89] It would be good to see more of this message from the environmental lobby.

Activists get a lot of publicity for their campaigns to make the oil majors run down their production rapidly. For instance, in May 2021, a Dutch court made a ruling aimed at forcing Shell to accelerate the reduction in its oil and gas production in a case brought by Friends of the Earth (FoE) among others. "Today an historic line has been drawn, no more spin, no more greenwashing, big oil is over", the FoE proclaimed. "Global polluters cannot continue their devastating operations".[90]

They are barking up the wrong tree. The reality is that Shell reducing its oil production will have no effect at all on global emissions. The real problem is us, the people who create the demand for oil. It is easier for environmental campaigners to go after "global polluters" than to recognise this fact. The problem is closer to home. Green NGOs have a vital role to play in persuading the public to change their behaviour.

Shell and other oil and gas majors do have an important part to play. As demand for oil and gas eventually declines, they could return their money to shareholders and fade away. To some extent, they are already on this path with large dividends and buy-back programmes. Some shareholders may be very happy with this. But it is definitely not the preferred option of senior executives who are motivated to secure the future of their companies. The majors are keen to carve out roles that will enable them to survive and thrive in the low-carbon world of the future.

Major oil and gas companies have exceptional potential to contribute to the energy transition. They have the financial resources and management, political, and technical skills to promote large international projects. They have offshore experience, they are experts in chemical processing, and they have close links with energy and chemical customers. Their initiatives could include installing electric charging points at petrol stations, using offshore and geological experience to promote offshore wind and carbon storage, and using financial and political skills to promote big low-carbon projects in the developing world. Shell is keen to turn itself into a supplier and trader of low-carbon energy.

BP's reaction to the energy shortages resulting from the war in Ukraine has been illuminating. BP has been a leader among major oil companies in energy transition. Announcing record profits in February 2023, Chief Executive Bernard Looney said, "The world wants and needs energy that is secure and affordable … We are helping to provide the energy that the world needs today … and … investing into the energy transition". He announced an increase of up to $1 billion p.a. in oil and gas as well as an increase in the same amount in investment in energy transition, including electric vehicle charging, hydrogen, renewables, and sustainable aviation fuels. BP's previous target of reducing emissions by 35–40% between 2019 and 2030 was reduced to 20–30%.[91] Environmentalists have criticised BP's intention to produce more oil but, in reality, BP's intention to increase their contribution to energy transition is much more significant. We should be urging the major oil companies to do more of this.

Some shareholders will no doubt question whether major oil and gas companies have the right skills to move into new low-carbon areas of business. There are certainly risks involved. Shareholders are anxiously watching the profitability of these new lines of business. We should encourage top management to take these risks. Government support is essential to open up the necessary commercial opportunities. BP's proposal for a pioneering large-scale CCS project at a gas power station on Teesside, now under review for government support, is an excellent example. BP first proposed a similar project at Peterhead more than 20 years ago, but the government failed to respond. That was a lost opportunity.

The oil industry has a big part to play. It is not entirely a bad thing that the chair of COP28 to be held in Dubai in 2023 is the CEO of a major oil company which also has a significant renewables business.

In spite of the COVID-19 crisis, 2021 was a record year for business jet traffic, which was 7% greater than in 2019, which was itself a record year. Business jets have the worst emissions, per passenger kilometre, of any form of transport. There are still plenty of businessmen out there who have not got the message!

Conclusion

Business is the key player in the energy transition. Business has to raise finance, develop and deploy advanced technology, and use marketing skills to persuade customers to adapt. Business is adaptable, inventive, and responsive to opportunities. Efforts to encourage business to provide information and to measure business performance on climate mitigation are going in the right direction, although this cannot be simplified. A lot of progress has been made, most major companies now take the issue of climate change seriously, and ambitious commitments are being made for the future. But the step change required to meet net zero has not yet occurred. That requires the intervention of government to make carbon saving profitable.

Public Opinion

Public opinion has to be prepared for the adaptations that will be required to reduce carbon emissions and for the cost. That is Key Policy No. 3. Governments and environmentalists have rightly divined that they need an optimistic story to sell to the public. But it is naïve to expect that the immense changes required to our way of life can be achieved, in the time available, without a certain amount of pain and significant cost. Eventually, the nettle will have to be grasped. The head of the UK's climate advisory group, the Climate Change Committee, recently criticised an "absolute refusal" by government ministers to "face the question of behavioural change".[92] Such an attitude is rapidly becoming inconsistent with the climate targets that the UK and others are setting. Yet the Climate Change Committee itself has done nothing to prepare the public for the challenges ahead, preferring to address its advice to the government, while reassuring the public that the costs are "manageable".

The committee's primary function is indeed to advise the government but it also has a statutory duty to involve the public in its work. Most of the areas in which the committee is rightly urging the government to move faster will depend on the public's willingness to change. While berating the government, the committee should also use its public platform to alert the public to the implications of the changes that it is pressing for.

Leaders need to acknowledge that there will be significant costs and that some changes will be inconvenient. But they can emphasise that the changes are necessary because of the extreme threat of climate change. Eventually, energy costs may indeed be lower and, after the adaptation, low-carbon energy may be convenient to use. Cities will be nicer places, with cleaner air and less traffic noise and smell. There will be wider local environmental benefits. And the economy will have adapted successfully to a changing world in which advanced low-carbon technologies are at the cutting edge of business and trade. Leaders can rightly point to the sunlit uplands at the end of the transition. In the meanwhile, they will need to show that the costs and inconvenience will be shared in a way that is socially fair.

We are going to have to move out of our comfort zones. Governments are understandably first adopting measures that are low cost and do not require significant changes in behaviour. Some low-carbon technologies, as well as energy efficiency, are already economically as well as environmentally attractive. Nevertheless, making the transition in time is going to involve significant cost and inconvenience and we are all going to have to face up to that.

The costs of transition are modest in relation to the benefits of saving the planet, and indeed other long-term benefits, but in terms of day-to-day national budgetary management, they look substantial. In the UK, the Climate Change Committee estimates the resource cost of its net zero scenario at 1–2% of GDP p.a. from now to 2050. That is about £20–40 billion p.a. The investment costs rise rapidly in the next few years and then they are largely recouped from about 2030 in reduced fuel costs for vehicles.[93]

As described above, the green NGOs and campaign groups have a vital role in preparing citizens to make necessary changes in their lifestyles. Environmental bodies have a tendency to concentrate on criticising big business, especially energy companies. It's their meat and drink and it's inside their comfort zone. It's much less popular to tell the general public that we will have to change our ways, but that is the real lever for change. Civil society influencers should be braver and more willing to tell the general public that we also have to adapt.

Without public support, it is very difficult for governments, of whatever complexion, to take firm action. The public's willingness to adapt, or otherwise, will be decisive. Governments can only regulate, impose or allow higher prices, or raise taxes, where there is a critical threshold of public acceptance. That is where the leadership of politicians, environmental organisations, and other high-profile influencers will be so important. The line that change will be cost-free and without inconvenience, and that it is only misguided government and big business that stand in the way, is not going to wear. Persuading the public of the need to adapt is the third key policy highlighted in this book.

The willingness of the public to adapt, or otherwise, directly impacts on the affordability, and feasibility of climate transitions. Take two of the main challenges facing the UK: the need to switch from gas central heating to heat pumps, and the need to electrify transport. Heat pumps are more expensive than gas boilers. They do not provide such intense heat and may require modifications to existing buildings. Electric cars are more costly than petrol or diesel ones, and owners have to get over their "range anxiety". The government cannot regulate unless the public is prepared to acquiesce. This is partly a question of the progress of the technology, including cost reduction, as already discussed. But it also depends on how seriously the public is taking the climate threat and whether they recognise that their own consumption patterns are part of the problem and will need to change. There is a certain amount of inconvenience in making these transitions. There is also the question of cost. It is inevitable that the government will have to pay most or all of the costs of low-income families. If middle-class families can be persuaded to bear their own costs, that will greatly reduce the burden on the public purse. If not, these are big budget items and their timing is going to be subject to tough scrutiny by government finance departments.

In the UK, the Uxbridge by-election of July 2023 has put this issue at the centre of national politics.[94] The Labour Party Mayor of London is extending his low-emission zone to the suburbs. It's very unpopular. It means that a lot of commuters, small business people, and family motorists will have to buy more modern and less polluting vehicles at considerable expense. Both the main political parties agree that this is what caused the Conservative Party to win the election, strongly against the voting trends in the nation as a whole. The party leaders are coming under pressure to ease back on green policies. "The lesson is surely that green policies are very unpopular when there's a direct cost to people", said Lord David Frost, a Conservative former Minister for Brexit. He has urged the Prime Minister to "re-think" the timetable for switching to electric cars and domestic heat pumps. The silence of the environmental lobby on this sensitive issue is deafening. This is not unique to the UK. Similar popular resistance is being experienced in Germany and elsewhere in Europe to regulations that will outlaw conventional vehicles and gas central heating.

This partly underlines the need to persuade the public that climate mitigation will require tough choices. But it isn't as simple as that. Part of the problem is that the cost of phasing out old vehicles falls disproportionately on the less well-off. They are the people running the old cars. Delaying the regulations switching to low-carbon alternatives is not an option because existing plans are barely sufficient to get to net zero by 2050. Governments will need to consider policies that share the burden more equitably with taxpayers or perhaps with motorists as a whole. Getting the balance of these policies right is a sensitive and critical issue. But none of these policies will work unless the public is on board.

The need to phase out gas central heating is coming to a head in Germany.[95] In April 2023, the German Cabinet approved a bill that bans most new oil and gas heating from 2024. This is partly an environmental measure. It is also intended to help cope with the loss of Russian gas. However, polls show that 78% of Germans are opposed to the plan. It looks as though there is a political struggle in store.

Public opinion on the climate threat now seems to be moving in the right direction. Campaigns such as Extinction Rebellion have certainly helped to raise awareness. The actual manifestations of climate change are becoming more evident in all parts of the world and no doubt this has been a factor. A recent large-scale international opinion survey by the United Nations Development Programme has shown that a majority of people across the globe see climate change as an emergency. For some regions and major countries, the figures were: the UK 81%, Western Europe 75–81%, Japan 79%, Australia 72%, the US 65%, Russia 65%, Brazil 64%, and India 59%. The more highly educated were likely to be concerned about climate change and to support policies for emissions reduction more.[96] The survey does not include China. However, according to an article in China Dialogue, 94% of respondents to a national survey in 2017 said that climate change was happening and 66% believe that it is mostly caused by human activities. The article says that Chinese attitudes to climate change are being driven by high-profile government campaigns and concerns about air pollution.[97]

It is a big step from recognising the emergency to accepting some degree of cost and inconvenience in daily life. There is a famous story about President Kennedy addressing a group of students during the Vietnam War. "Who thinks we should have an all volunteer army?" he asked. Every hand was raised. "Who would volunteer?", he continued. Not a single hand. We are going to have to face up to the practical consequences for ordinary citizens of our green ambitions.

Chapter 4

Government Policies: Fair and Effective Incentives and Obligations

Key Policy No. 4.

Strong regulatory action by governments is Key Policy No. 4. Governments need to apply a judicious blend of carbon levies, financial support, regulation, and persuasion. Local circumstances will determine the options that are most effective and most acceptable to the public. For developing countries, it will be vital to attract international investment capital. Donor nations and international development banks must help. Their aim should be, in partnership with host countries, to create the conditions where private capital will flow.

Action by Governments

Governments have four main intervention options. They can tax, or price, carbon emissions in one way or another, they can provide financial support for specific technologies, they can regulate to require businesses and customers to choose low-carbon options, and they can try to change behaviour through information and exhortation. Governments have to work out which combination of these options will be most cost-effective and can win public support.

The rest of this chapter makes general comments about each of these options. Then it reviews, in broad outline, the policies that have been adopted by some salient countries, the US, China, the EU, the UK, India, South Africa, Indonesia, and Nigeria. Finally, it will draw some conclusions.

Carbon Taxes

Industry and some environmentalists are calling for governments to put a price on carbon emissions through carbon taxes or trading schemes. In theory, this is the most efficient way to achieve emissions reductions.

There are some very strong economic arguments in favour of carbon taxes. They provide across the board incentives to reduce emissions. Industry, and business in general, knows much better than government what low-carbon options it has and what they cost, and if the incentives are there business will be creative. Carbon taxes provide economic clarity for business planning and investment. For these reasons, carbon taxation is favoured by many businessmen[98] and economists,[99] as well as some environmentalists.

Carbon taxes can be levied at a fixed rate or they can take the form of cap and trade mechanisms. In cap and trade, businesses are given, or have to buy, quotas of emissions. If their emissions exceed their quotas, they have to buy more. But if they are able to emit less than their quotas they have a valuable asset to sell.

The beauty of quota trading is that it should ensure that the least cost carbon-saving options are adopted not just within individual companies but across the whole trading system. Companies for whom the cost of reducing emissions would be very high can buy credits. Companies with low-cost-carbon saving options can profit. Perhaps for this reason, cap and trade systems, such as the European Union's Emissions Trading System (ETS), have been the most popular form of carbon taxation thus far.

These two main options, taxation at a flat rate versus carbon trading, have different economic consequences, at least in theory. In the case of a flat rate carbon tax, governments know the maximum burden on industry, but not the extent of carbon emissions saving. In the case of a cap and trading system, governments know by how much carbon emissions will be reduced, but not the price of quotas in the market and, therefore, the burden on industry. In practice, over time, there is a degree of convergence because, whichever system is chosen, governments tend to make adjustments to achieve their overall objectives both for carbon saving and for the burden on industry.

Carbon taxes sound like a great idea. Let the polluters, assumed to be the big industrial energy companies and oil and gas producers, pay. Not only are emissions reduced but the government raises money that could be spent on other low-carbon incentives. The reality is not quite so attractive. The costs inevitably flow through to consumers, raising the price of things that bulk large in the budgets of poorer and middle-income families, that is to say, electricity and gas, transport, and the manufacture and distribution of goods of all kinds including food. Carbon taxes are highly "regressive". They hit the less well-off hardest and raise serious questions of social justice. Politicians tend not to be as enthusiastic as economists.

There is an obvious solution to this problem, which is to devote some or all of the proceeds of a carbon tax to compensate poor consumers. Many schemes of this nature have been put forward. For instance, in 2017 some very senior Republicans in the US proposed that the proceeds of a carbon tax would be paid out equally to all households in the US as what they called a "carbon dividend".[100] Almost all relatively low pay households would be better off overall under such a scheme.

The "Green New Deal" proposed in the US and in the UK is a much broader approach to the same problem.[101] The idea is to combine carbon taxes, or other climate measures, with a much wider programme of social reform.

The scope of the US Democratic Party's proposals was breathtaking. According to the Council on Foreign Relations,[102] it included the following:

- *Emissions*: cutting net greenhouse gas emissions to zero over 10 years.
- *Manufacturing*: spurring "massive growth in clean manufacturing".
- *Power use*: meeting all US power demand "through clean, renewable, and zero-emission energy sources".
- *Agriculture*: sharply reducing emissions and other pollution from agriculture.
- *Infrastructure*: upgrading infrastructure, including transportation and housing, and ensuring all infrastructure bills considered by Congress address climate change.
- *Jobs*: guaranteeing a job with a "family-sustaining wage" for everyone.

- *Welfare and social justice*: providing everyone in the United States with high-quality health care, affordable housing, economic security, clean water, clean air, and healthy food, while addressing systemic social exclusion and injustice.

Some of these ideas have come through in President Biden's Infrastructure Investment and Jobs Act and his Inflation Reduction Act but they cannot be said to have measured up to the last two, very ambitious, bullets.

The fundamental problem with "tax and dividend" is that taxes are unpopular and trust in government is often low. If even a few low-income people are worse off, they will get a lot of attention. It is notoriously costly, in any scheme of tax reform, to ensure that absolutely everyone is better off. Money spent on relieving the social impact of carbon taxes will not be available for low-carbon investments.

Carbon taxes are very efficient at promoting low-carbon options that are already available and close to being competitive. They are not so good at bringing in new technologies that are far from being commercial today, because very high tax rates would be required to get them through the initial stages of demonstration and mass deployment. Incentives targeted on specific technologies are likely to be more cost-effective.

Carbon taxes, and to some extent all policies that place burdens on industry, pose the question of what to do about industries that face international competition, such as iron and steel companies. That is why, in the ETS, the iron and steel industry, among others, receives free quotas based on historic emissions, whereas the power industry, which faces little competition outside the EU, has to buy its quotas. Handing out free quotas blunts the edge of cap and trade. In theory, emitters still have the incentive to reduce emissions and have valuable spare quotas to sell. In practice, the option exists to carry on as before without economic penalty. Also, if the industry treats the price of quotas as a marginal cost of production, there may be a profitable opportunity to raise prices. The polluters are rewarded! For these reasons, the European Union is keen to make all emitters buy their quotas. But to do so, they have to address the problem of international competition.

Hence, the proposals in the EU, and also in the US, for putting a tax on the carbon content of imports are known as a Carbon Border Tax. The idea is that this tax will burden imports by no more than the burden that climate policies place on domestic producers, leading to fair terms of trade. Nevertheless, border carbon taxes are highly controversial. Developing countries see them as an attempt to impose the climate policies of developed importing countries on them and as a barrier to their trade and growth opportunities. They regard these taxes as a violation of the principle of "common but differentiated responsibilities" enshrined in the Climate Treaty, under which developed countries are expected to take a leading role and go ahead of the developing world in the adoption of climate measures. They are seen as just the sort of "disguised restriction on international trade" that the treaty warns against. So, Carbon Border Taxes have become a further controversial element in climate geopolitics.

Carbon border taxes are beginning to seem inevitable, but they should only be introduced through a process of negotiation with those developing countries most affected and in association with programmes to help those countries to manufacture with lower emissions. The topic is discussed further below.

Financial Support

Financial support, more or less closely targeted to particular technologies, has proved highly effective in getting new technologies over the barrier of mass adoption and driving down costs. The most obvious examples of this are solar PV and wind power.

Solar PV benefited from massive subsidies, especially in Germany, in the early years of this century in the form of guaranteed prices called "feed in tariffs". These subsidies ultimately led to mass adoption and a 90% fall in price. There has been no breakthrough in the technology, which remains essentially the same. However, large-scale production and the streamlining of installation has driven down the cost spectacularly. Solar power promises to be the leading low-carbon energy technology of the future.

Wind energy has been through a similar process with big government subsidies starting in Denmark, and costs falling by at least 50%. The costs of offshore wind, also seen as an expensive option at first, have also fallen sharply, largely as a result of promotion first by Denmark and then by the UK. This has led to a staggering increase in the size of individual turbines and a tenfold increase in unit generating capacity since the 1990s. The latest offshore turbines being installed on the UK's Dogger Bank are 248 metres tall, not so far short of the Eiffel Tower at 330 metres, and each with a generating capacity of 14 Mw.

These subsidies can now be judged as having been successful because they have enabled wind and solar power to become economically competitive and enter the mainstream of electricity supply in many parts of the world. They were not always seen so positively at the time. In the early days of PV adoption, when costs were high, many regarded the German subsidies as extremely wasteful. The UK also took a big risk in subsidising offshore wind at a time when it still looked expensive.

We need to accelerate our spending on wind and solar power, but this must go hand in hand with investment in the technologies that can provide back-up and which are generally less well advanced, otherwise there is an unacceptable risk to security of supply.

Governments may hope, by supporting low-carbon advanced technologies, not only to mitigate climate change but also to promote profitable new domestic industries. This worked for Denmark. As a result of being an early promoters, Denmark is now one of the world's leading manufacturers of wind generators. But it didn't work for Germany or the UK. The manufacture of solar PV units has largely passed to low-cost suppliers, especially in China. The UK's offshore wind generators are still mainly supplied by Danish and German companies.

The massive subsidies for clean energy in President Biden's Inflation Reduction Act are conditional on high proportions of US made content. That is intended to ensure that US industry benefits, with associated jobs, but it raises major questions of international trade policy and may harm relations with the developing world and other exporting countries. The "buy American" rule may also raise costs and slow the rate of transition. This is discussed further below.

To varying degrees, giving subsidies for specific technologies involves governments in "picking winners". It's a phrase that got a bad reputation in the UK in the 1980s when the government, under the slogan "white heat of technology", made big investments in areas such as nuclear power and aviation. These turned out to be blind alleys and a lot of money was wasted. It was not so much that there was anything wrong with the technologies but the timing was wrong, or there was misjudgement of the UK's role in global technology development.

For instance, the UK invested heavily in advanced nuclear technologies such as sodium-cooled fast reactors, gas-cooled high-temperature reactors, and nuclear fuel reprocessing in the 1970s and 1980s. At that time, there was a widespread expectation that nuclear power would dominate future electricity generation and that uranium would be in short supply. Then came the Chernobyl nuclear accident, cheap gas, and the development of the highly efficient combined cycle gas turbine. Gas became the preferred technology for a generation and the UK was left with unwanted research and demonstration projects and a huge bill for nuclear clean-up.

The UK did develop and build its own unique design of gas cooled nuclear power stations which have significant safety benefits. After a dire construction phase, these Advanced Gas-cooled Reactors (AGRs) have performed well and they still provide nearly 10% of the UK's electricity today. But the rest of the world followed a different course, building mainly US-designed Pressurised Water Reactors (PWRs). Eventually, the UK fell in line. The French began by licensing American PWR designs and have developed a much more successful nuclear industry. Now, a French company, EDF, is building PWR reactors in the UK. There is nothing to show for decades of UK government investment.

Ironically, now that climate change threatens and the war in Ukraine has disrupted the gas supply, many countries are once more looking at the potential of fast reactors and high-temperature reactors. But the UK has decommissioned its research sites and is no longer in a leading position.

Similarly, in the 1970s and 1980s, the UK developed a variety of advanced commercial and military aeroplanes. But it became clear that the UK, on its own, simply did not have the resources to compete internationally as an aircraft manufacturer. Rolls-Royce is still a successful aero-engine manufacturer and the UK has a large aeronautical industry, but today the UK buys military jets from the US, and Boeing and Airbus dominate the manufacture of airliners.

In these examples, government money was spent on very specific technologies. The Inflation Reduction Act and the range of subsidies available in the EU are spread so widely across a range of low-carbon technologies that the risks of "picking winners" are much reduced. Equally, no individual technology is supercharged with highly focused support.

The moral to be drawn from the UK's experience of the 1970s is clear. We cannot afford to draw the conclusion, as some have done, that governments should never pick winners. But careful and realistic consideration is needed as to how national initiatives fit into the global picture, and for a country the size of the UK, this will often point to international collaboration.

Government spending on research, development and initial deployment is vital. With the right incentives, industry can be relied upon to invest in technologies that are close to becoming commercial, but only government is able to invest on a large scale in technologies that are at an earlier stage. Many of the technologies that have contributed most to emissions reduction have their origins or have achieved major advances in government research laboratories, especially in the US. One of the best things to come out of the Paris Climate Summit in 2015 was the commitment of leading nations to double their research spending on clean energy under the heading "Mission Innovation".

Nobody can be sure of how much costs will come down as advanced technologies move to production at scale. To varying degrees, they are in competition with each other. For instance, hydrogen competes with heat pumps to provide low-carbon domestic heating. Hydrogen also competes with fossil fuels plus carbon storage to provide backup for renewables. And hydrogen competes with electric batteries and biofuels to power heavy vehicles. The need for low-carbon energy will be so enormous, and the requirements so diverse, that probably there will be a need for all the main technologies under development today. Nevertheless, there are risks in making big investments in specific technologies, and those risks will have to be accepted. Not every country has to develop its own technology and international cooperation can help to manage these risks. Governments have to decide where to try to develop their own technology and where technology is better acquired from other players.

Regulation

Government regulation has been highly successful in improving the efficiency of appliances, vehicles, and buildings in the US, EU, and elsewhere. There is no direct cost to the government and major specific results can be achieved. The cost falls on domestic or industrial consumers and depends on the available options for compliance.

The potential for reducing emissions through regulation is closely linked to the progress of technology, business investment, and also to public attitudes. The EU Commission proposes to ban new petrol and diesel cars from 2035. The UK intended to ban them from 2030, but has now also set the date at 2035. These targets can only be achieved if electric or possibly hydrogen vehicles are close to being cost competitive, if industry invests in manufacturing capacity, if charging points are sufficiently ubiquitous, and if the public accepts that this change with its associated costs and inconvenience is necessary.

Governments face an even more difficult challenge in reducing and eventually eliminating gas central heating, where it is not yet clear that affordable and effective alternatives are available. The UK has said that it will ban the installation of gas boilers in new houses from 2025 and that it is "setting the ambition" of banning the installation of new gas boilers in existing houses from 2035.[103] Since boilers last for around 15 years, that is the last date consistent with zero emissions by 2050. The government say that its transition plan "focuses on reducing bills and improving comfort". That would require remarkable technological progress or large government subsidies. The government should be a little more honest about the implications of its policy, which seems likely to provide a critical test of the public's willingness to adapt.

In the UK, transport, mainly cars, accounts for 31% of total CO_2 emissions and the residential sector, which is mainly gas central heating, accounts for 17%.[104] So tackling some 50% of UK emissions today depends on the success of tough government regulations to end reliance on gas boilers and petrol or diesel cars. The situation in other developed northern hemisphere countries in Europe and North America is similar.

Governments have to take the necessary steps to win public support. These include investing in the infrastructure necessary to make low-carbon alternatives reasonably convenient. They also include subsidies or other measures to protect the less well-off and convince the public that the impact on the various sections of society is fair.

Governments may hope that the conversion of industry to clean energy can largely be achieved through some form of taxation on carbon emissions. But this also will probably require tough regulation at some stage.

Information and Persuasion

In a free and open society, the government's powers of persuasion are fairly limited. Other influencers, including environmental NGOs, may be more effective, especially if they enjoy a higher level of trust. Much depends on the circumstances, especially the extent to which the public shares the government's objectives. In Japan, after the Fukushima nuclear accident, when all nuclear power stations were shut down, the government was very successful in persuading people to cut down on electricity consumption. That was, at least in part, because everyone recognised that there was a national emergency. It also reflected the strong cultural cohesion of Japanese society.

In 2010, the UK government set up a "Behavioural Insights Team", popularly known as the "Nudge Unit", inside the Cabinet Office, to "apply behavioural science to public policy". The concept was based on the work of the Nobel-Prize winning economist, Richard Thaler. It worked on green topics, including improving energy efficiency, among others. Success was unspectacular. The team still exists, but now it is an independent consultancy rather than a part of government.

In the UK, the government's ability to influence behaviour is limited by the relatively low level of trust that government agencies enjoy and by public aversion to what has been called the "nanny state". It is also a problem, discussed elsewhere, that environmental NGOs concentrate on attacking big corporations and are much less willing to try to influence public behaviour.

If all that seems rather negative, public information, especially when linked to financial or regulatory schemes, is an essential part of the armoury of all governments in pursuing climate policies. Hopefully, as the impact of climate change becomes ever more acute and awareness of the climate crisis increases the public will become more receptive to government influence.

Conclusion on Government Policy

Government intervention is essential if we are to get anywhere near to net zero by 2050. Climate taxes, financial support, regulation, and influence are all needed to achieve big reductions in carbon emissions. None is a panacea on its own. Getting the mix right is critical for the success of government climate policies. This is partly a question of economics, but it is also, to a large degree, a question of national culture and what the public is most willing to accept. The public has to be convinced that policies are fair, and this may require well judged support to mitigate the impact on the less well off. It is understandable that governments do not want to alarm the public but honesty about the challenges ahead is essential to prepare public opinion. The need for firm regulatory action by governments is Key Policy No. 4.

Government Climate Regulation in Selected Countries

Government policies have to be adapted to national circumstances, and these differ widely. The following sections outline and critique the policies of a range of nations, the US, China, the EU, the UK, India, South Africa, Indonesia, and Nigeria, chosen to contrast the different issues faced by economies at various stages of development as well as to include the largest emitters and potential emitters.

Chart V.

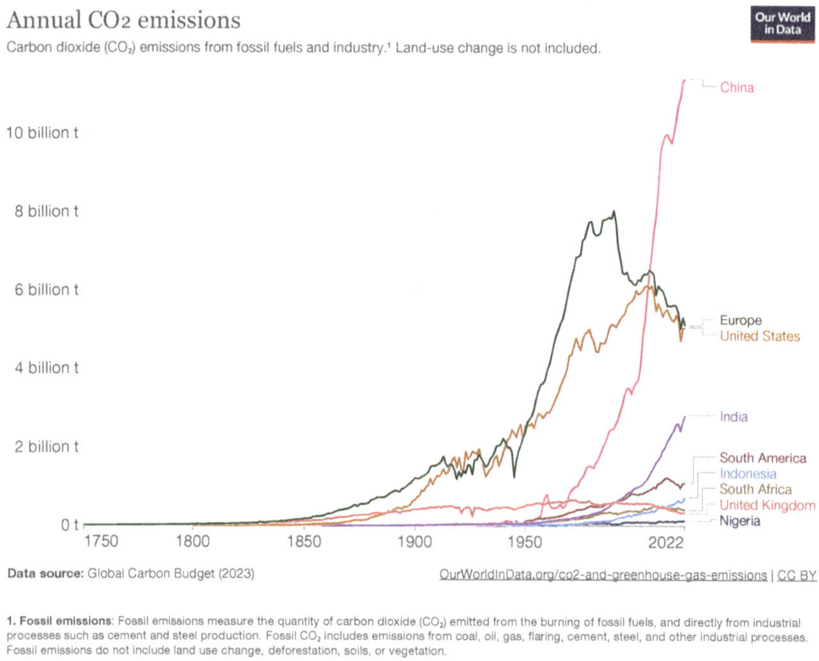

Chart V shows the emissions records of these countries. It shows that the emissions of developed nations are in decline. Those of China and India have risen rapidly, while those of other developing nations are beginning what could, in the absence of low-carbon policies, become similarly rapid increases.

Chart VI shows the emissions of the same nations on a per capita basis. China no longer appears such an outlier, with emissions per person that are less than those of the US and not very different from the EU. The US is the largest emitter per head of major economies. India's emissions per head are modest compared to those of the developed countries.

Chart VI.

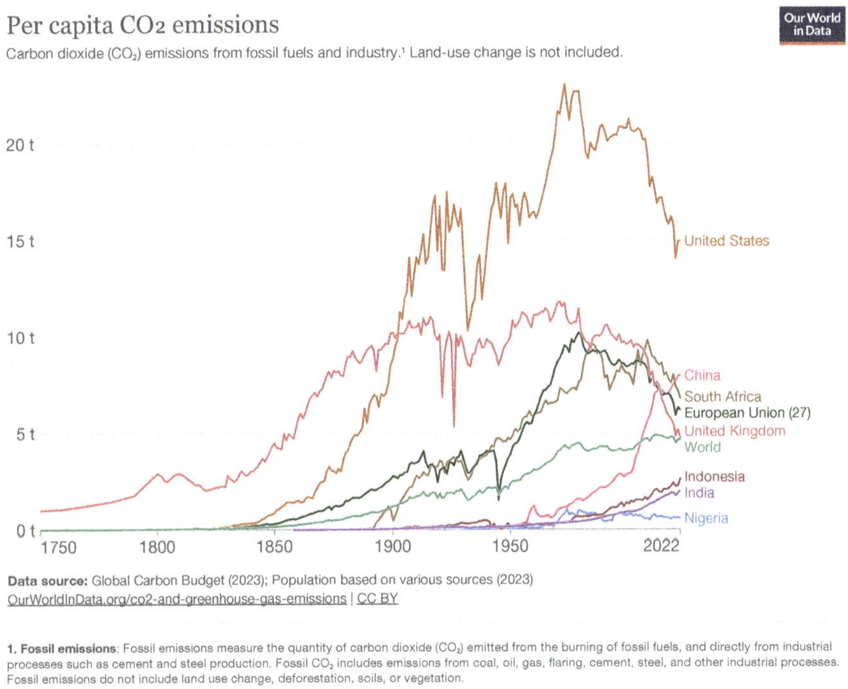

The US

US CO_2 emissions peaked at around 6 Gt in the early years of this century, before declining to 4.7 Gt in 2021, a reduction of about 17%. They now account for about 14% of global CO_2 emissions, making the US the second largest emitter after China. Emissions per person are significantly higher than the average for the OECD and about twice the level of China. However, emissions per unit of GDP are roughly in line with the developed OECD countries as a whole and less than half those of China.[105] The US has set targets to reduce emissions by 50%, compared to 2005, by 2030, and to net zero by 2050.

President Biden has embarked on a massive spending programme supporting the deployment of low-carbon energy technologies and the building of necessary infrastructure. The Federal government also spends heavily on low-carbon energy R&D. It sets standards for the efficiency of vehicles and appliances and it issues guidance on the efficiency of buildings.

However, the shape of government climate policies in the US is influenced by the division of powers between Congress, the President, the Supreme Court, and state governments and by the lack of consensus between Democrats and Republicans. The US Federal government controls the wholesale marketing of electricity and inter-state transmission, but the states regulate their own power generation and distribution.

Repeated efforts by Democratic congressmen and senators to promote Federal carbon taxes or trading mechanisms have failed to gain the necessary majorities in Congress. However cap and trade has flourished at state level. New York and 10 other states have a joint carbon trading mechanism and California has its own scheme.

In 2015 President Obama proposed a cap and trade plan for state power station emissions, designed to achieve a gradual shift away from coal, to be enforced by the Environmental Protection Agency (EPA). Twenty-seven states objected. The Supreme Court delayed implementation and eventually ruled that, in the absence of a specific Congressional mandate, the EPA did not have the necessary powers. In the meantime, the scheme had been axed by the Republican administration of President Trump.

America's aims for emissions reduction have become more credible with the passage of President Biden's two big spending acts: the Infrastructure Investment and Jobs Act (IIJA), and the, curiously named, Inflation Reduction Act (IRA). The IIJA provides $1.2 trillion for a wide range of investments that include charging points for electric vehicles, upgrading the power grid, energy efficiency, and building electrification. The IRA provides $369 billion for the development and deployment of clean energy technologies. These include wind and solar as well as hydrogen, energy storage, carbon capture use and storage, and nuclear power. The incentives largely take the form of direct subsidies, such as tax credits, for projects to be carried out by the private sector. The impact of these subsidies will be immense. The support for clean energy is worth 30% of investment costs or, alternatively, 2.5 cents per kWh, which is about half the IEA's estimate of PV generation costs. However President Biden's original intent to include far-reaching social reforms in the act did not survive congressional scrutiny.

The IRA is motivated in part by the desire to rebuild America's manufacturing industries and, for reasons of national security, to counter China's growing dominance of climate technology. Most of the support is conditional on manufacturing in the US. This has profound implications. It drives a coach and horses through established international trading rules that the US has previously promoted internationally as part of the "Washington consensus". The US has changed tack now that its own industries are at risk. This has triggered an international arms race on climate-related economic measures, as Europe and other developed regions rush to protect their climate-related industries with their own major subsidies. This may give a boost to climate investment in the West, but it raises the drawbridge on trade in climate products with the developing world. The implications of such acts of climate nationalism are discussed in Chapter 4.

Because of the need for consensus in Congress, the IRA also includes provisions that guarantee a minimum level of oil and gas licensing on Federal lands.

The spread of support offered in the Inflation Reduction Act is very wide, and it will be for business to decide how much to invest in the different technologies. The risk of "picking winners" has largely been avoided but possibly at the expense of progress for the less commercial technologies.

The more progressive US states have much more prescriptive policies than the Federal government, with California and New York in the lead. A majority of the states have renewable portfolio standards. In other words, they specify the share of electricity generation that must be renewable. California says that 60% of electricity must be renewable by 2030. State regulation is not as watertight as Federal regulation would be and, of course, not as comprehensive. California has a law banning the sale of new petrol cars from 2035, but there is no such requirement at Federal level.

The US National Laboratories have an impressive record of technical innovation and the Department of Energy, which runs them, spends more than $10 billion p.a. on clean energy research, development and deployment. This puts the US in the same league as the EU and China, who are the other biggest spenders on clean energy research and development.

US coal consumption has approximately halved since reaching its peak in 2008, mainly as a result of cheap gas and renewables, and this has been one of the main reasons why total emissions have declined. Gas consumption grew rapidly in recent years but dipped over the COVID-19 period. Oil consumption may now be about to decline, but is still close to peak levels. Since the reductions that have been achieved in power generation, transport is now the biggest US emitter, having increased by 13% since 1990.[106]

US government contributions to international climate finance are also bedevilled by the division of powers. President Biden promised to contribute $11.4 billion in 2022, but Congress voted around $1 billion,[107] far from adequate as a US contribution to the $100 billion p.a. from 2020 that the developed world promised at the Copenhagen Climate Summit.

The Biden administration's financial support will supercharge business investment in clean energy over the next few years. Through its massive government R&D investments and outstanding facilities the US will certainly be a leader in technical innovation. This focus on positive incentives for new technology reflects the US culture and constitution. Can the US spend its way to net zero? It is doubtful. Somehow the US has to get over its addiction to oil and the internal combustion engine. To achieve net zero, the US will almost certainly eventually need to adopt tougher regulatory policies and carbon taxation in some form, areas in which the Federal government is relatively weak today, but where individual states, such as California and New York, are already in the vanguard. Opinion formers in the powerful environmental NGOs need to prepare public opinion. New legislation now being proposed on vehicle emissions standards may lead the way.

China

China consumes more than half the world's coal, produces more than half of the world's steel, aluminium, and cement, and contributes about 20%

of global CO_2 emissions. It is by far the world leader in hydro, wind, and solar power and in electric vehicles. So the success of China's low-carbon policies matters a lot.

China has many of the resources of developed nations but it still has a large population living in relative poverty. Weaning China from coal is a top priority for climate mitigation. It isn't easy to achieve, bearing in mind that China's energy needs are still growing rapidly. It's a task that only the Chinese government can perform and other countries will not be able to exert much influence.

The West would like China to bring forward its target that emissions will peak by 2030. But this is easier said than done, bearing in mind China's quest for energy security and need for rapid economic growth. The former Prime Minister Johnson assured the British people that there is no need for "hair shirts", but are we implicitly asking Chinese people to wear them?

China has a complex set of interests involved in its climate policies. China now recognises that its unbridled economic growth of recent decades has caused immense damage to the environment. This is most evident to visitors in the poor air quality of major cities, such as Beijing, Shanghai, and Wuhan. But the pollution of land, rivers, and the coast is, arguably, even more serious. President Xi Jinping came near to admitting the problem in his address to the Party Congress of 2017 when he said, "There has been a clear shift away from the tendency to neglect ecological and environmental protection" and promised to "promote a revolution in energy production and consumption and build an energy sector that is clean, low-carbon, safe and efficient".[108]

In China, the need to clean up the local environment and the need to protect the global atmosphere are regarded as parts of the same ecological challenge. Some, though not all of the solutions are the same. The adoption of renewables and of electric vehicles with renewable generation, and the promotion of energy efficiency will help the global as well as the local environment. But moving coal-powered industry away from cities, de-sulphurising the flues of coal power stations, or coal gasification, will not.

China is, by far, the world's biggest producer of solar PV and wind energy. China has 85% of the world's rare earth processing capacity and manufactures 80% of the world's battery cells. China is also the world's largest manufacturer of electric vehicles, with almost half of world production. For China, continuing to develop and deploy these technologies is good for the economy and export trade, and it is good for China's international leadership and soft power. China has powerful economic and geopolitical motives for developing its low-carbon technology.

Related to this, China has a more general need to rebalance its economy. China has achieved spectacular growth over the past 30 years by investing in heavy industry, manufacturing for export, and a vast construction programme. This has lifted living standards, at least in the cities, to the level of a middle ranking nation. However, breaking out of this level and moving towards the level of fully developed advanced economies has proved notoriously difficult for many countries. It means shifting the balance of the economy from basic heavy manufacturing towards high value-added high-tech industries and services. Shifting to a low-carbon economy can certainly help to accelerate this trend. Thus, to a certain degree, policies for climate mitigation can be seen as part of China's broader strategy for taking the next step in economic development.

Besides these positive incentives, China has a more defensive reason for wanting to go green, and especially to adopt electric vehicles.

China has to import about 70% of its oil requirements and 40% of its gas. As tensions with the West increase, this is a critical strategic vulnerability, especially as about half of the oil is imported from the Middle East via the Straits of Hormuz and Malacca, both of which are dominated, in military terms, by the US Navy. China may reflect on the problems that Europe is experiencing, following the invasion of Ukraine, with its dependence on Russian gas. China is trying to diversify its oil supply, for instance, by increasing imports by pipeline from Russia, which it may consider more secure. But demand for personal mobility in China is growing rapidly. Unless China can moderate oil demand through rapid investment in electric vehicles and public transport, continued and growing dependence on Middle East imports seems inevitable. This provides a strong incentive for China to pursue low-carbon transport policies.

Because of the rapid economic growth required to continue the improvement in China's living standards, and consequent increase in energy supply, China has to run fast simply to stand still on CO_2 emissions. That is approximately what it is doing, with its immense investment in renewables just about sufficient to meet demand growth but not, so far, to achieve any significant reduction in the underlying demand for fossil fuels.

China uses many of the same policy instruments as the West, notably feed-in tariffs, quotas, fiscal incentives, regulation, and government spending, to promote low-carbon policies. However, the whole is governed by the highly centralised system of Communist Party control in which officials at provincial and local levels are held to account for successful delivery of government policy aims.

At the highest level of this pyramid is the Five-Year Plan. The current, 14th plan, runs from 2021 to 2025. It contains some positive messages on climate change. It says that China has, "shifted direction towards a phase of higher quality development" and that "we will promote the energy revolution, and build a clean, low-carbon, safe, and efficient energy system".[109]

The targets are to reduce energy consumption per unit of GDP by 13.5% over the five years, and CO_2 emissions per GDP by 18%, showing that the biggest reductions will come from energy efficiency and structural change in the economy rather than the shift from fossil fuels to renewables. This is consistent with no reduction, or even some increase, in the absolute level of CO_2 emissions, given the expected increase in GDP over the period. China's longer term targets are that emissions will peak by 2030, or earlier if possible, and then fall to net zero by 2060.

Coal accounts for about 70% of China's CO_2 emissions. Coal is relied upon to provide energy security at a time of rapidly growing electricity demand and increasing deployment of variable renewables. In the main coal provinces, coal mining and power generation are big contributors to employment and GDP growth. This makes it socially and politically difficult to cut these industries back. The plan says that China will, "reasonably control the scale and development pace of coal power construction, and promote replacement of coal with electricity". That provides a fair description of the stance of Chinese policymakers on coal today. Dependence on coal is being moderated but there is no urgent cutback.

Part of the problem is that the market for electricity is heavily constrained. Provinces like to keep the generation of their power needs to themselves, and the running order of power stations generally is administered to deliver "fair shares" of generating time. This tends to protect coal. A more flexible system should enable renewables, which are usually the lowest cost option, to displace coal more rapidly. Integrating the grids of different provinces could help to manage the variability of renewables.

China is taking steps towards opening up wholesale electricity markets and has introduced an ETS for power stations. However, the trading schemes are still being tested and the ETS is designed in such a way as not to incentivise switching from coal to gas or renewables. The government evidently feels that it has to protect the coal industry from rapid change.

Turning to China's international policies, China's immense Belt and Road programme of international investment, which has a large energy element, is discussed in Chapter 5. Although environmental guidance has been issued, the programme is not primarily directed to emissions reduction and has financed fossil fuel power stations. China recently announced that it would no longer finance new coal power stations abroad, a major step forward for the world climate outlook.

China has many positive low-carbon policies and is making a leading contribution to the development and deployment of renewables. China faces a tough task in changing the direction of its vast coal-dependent economy while still maintaining rapid economic growth and energy security. Progress is impressive but still not nearly fast enough to meet the 1.5°C global climate objective. China could consider opening up its power market to enable renewables to compete freely with coal and gas and reform its carbon trading regime so that there is a direct incentive to switch from coal generation to gas and renewables.

Under the Climate Treaty (UNFCCC), China has strictly maintained its position as a developing country, thereby avoiding the obligations that developed countries have to give climate support to other developing countries. China can point to the fact that its GDP per head is still less than half the average of the developed OECD countries and that China still has a large population of relatively poor people. But China is the second largest economy in the world and its participation would certainly add weight and cohesion to the support effort. One of the arguments most commonly used in the US and elsewhere in the West to resist climate policies is that China is not pulling its weight.

The European Union

Europe contributes 7.5% of global CO_2 emissions. Europe is a leader in the climate effort and its achievements are substantial. Regulation from Brussels is a powerful driver. Largely due to the contributions of renewables and nuclear power, Europe has significantly lower carbon intensity than other major developed economies.

Germany, the EU's largest economy, is still dependent on coal for more than a quarter of its electric power. That is astonishing given the high profile that the German government has given to its "energiewende" climate mission. The plan was not to phase this out until 2038, although the new coalition government is aiming for 2030. However, it was large subsidies in Germany that launched the phenomenal rise of solar electricity.

In the short term, in spite of impressive longer term climate targets, the EU has reacted to the energy crisis of the Ukraine war not only by achieving impressive reductions in gas demand but also by increasing coal consumption, subsidising gas supply, and investing in infrastructure for gas imports.

The EU's ETS is by far the largest in the world, leaving aside the Chinese scheme which is at a much earlier stage of development. For a long time, it has been plagued by industrial lobbying, over-generous granting of free quotas, and consequent very low-carbon prices. But more recent reforms have driven the CO_2 price up to €100 per tonne of CO_2, which, if sustained, is certainly enough to make a big difference.

The EU drives its carbon reduction programme through targets and national quotas, through its ETS, and through a wide range of other policies and financial programmes of which the €1 trillion Green Deal is the flagship.

In 2022, the member states agreed on an impressive package of new measures.[110] CO_2 emissions are to be reduced by 55% to 2030, from 1990, and to net zero by 2045, five years before global net zero is judged necessary by the IEA for achieving climate goals. There are targets for reductions in total energy consumption, in the emissions of industry, power and transport, and for the share of renewables. Free emissions quotas in the ETS are to be phased out by 2034. From 2027, parallel carbon markets for heating and for vehicles are to be introduced.

To protect industry from less regulated overseas competitors, a Carbon Border Adjustment Mechanism (CBAM) is to be phased in from 2023 to 2026. Initially, it will only apply to iron and steel, electricity, fertilisers, hydrogen, and cement, but eventually, it is expected to be expanded to cover all industries within the ETS. Exporting nations will have to purchase CBAM certificates covering the embedded carbon in their exports to the EU. The cost of the certificates will equal the price of carbon certificates in the ETS less the charge, if any, on carbon emissions in the exporting country. This is going to be intrusive and bureaucratic and highly resented by exporting developing nations.

CBAMs are part of a worrying trend towards climate nationalism in which major measures by developed nations to strengthen their climate industries create new barriers to trade with developing countries. America's IRA, already mentioned, could inhibit investment in Africa in low-carbon products for export to the US. Dialogue with the countries most affected is essential.

That is why several German government departments have proposed the formation of "International Climate Clubs"[111] in which participating rich and poor nations would agree on a package of mutually beneficial measures, including national carbon measures, rates of progress towards net zero, terms of carbon trade, and aid packages. The G7 announced the formation of such a club at their meeting in December 2022. It's an interesting idea discussed further below.

A "Social Climate Fund" of €87 billion will help to protect EU consumers from the impact of the trading schemes on heating and vehicles.

All this adds up to an impressive framework of regulation for achieving net zero, probably the most comprehensive of any major economy. But today, Europe is a long way from having the affordable technologies, the business strategies, and the public acceptance of change that will be needed to achieve the dramatic emissions reductions that the government planners are aiming for. This is especially true for industry, domestic, and commercial heating and cooling and to a lesser extent for transport. So the regulatory framework involves, necessarily, an act of faith that, with the support being provided, all the required changes will come together as necessary at the right time. Let us hope so.

Europe's energy security is much more directly threatened by the war in Ukraine than that of the US. In the short term, this is leading to a revival of coal generation and investment in gas infrastructure. Hopefully, these are short-term measures, but time is limited to establish a credible pathway towards net zero by 2050.

Compared to the US, Europe is strong on central government regulation by the Commission but has been weaker on finance. Europe will depend on a strong industrial response to regulatory signals including carbon pricing. Regulation is more likely to be successful in promoting the deployment of already competitive technologies, such as solar and wind, than it is in bringing forward less advanced technologies, such as hydrogen, carbon sequestration, and energy storage. Probably, the EU will need to increase the contribution of central EU finance to achieve its objectives. This may be about to happen as the EU faces up to the competitive impact of big subsidies for domestically manufactured green products in the US.

According to the European Commission,[112] the EU, its member states, and the European Investment Bank are together the world's biggest contributors to international public climate finance, contributing €23.4 billion in 2020. They are also the world's largest provider of development assistance, including climate aid, providing €67 billion in 2020. There are issues, discussed elsewhere, over how much of this money goes into bilateral deals involving EU exports and how much goes into international funds over which the developing nations share control. Nevertheless, this is a major contribution. If the EU seeks to enter into climate clubs with developing nations, development aid will inevitably be a part of the equation.

The EU is a leader in low-carbon energy transition. Europe has made a major contribution to the commercialisation of renewables through feed-in tariffs and its ETS is now beginning to bite. Investment in less commercial technology has been less impressive, but this may be about to change as Europe reacts to the challenge posed by America's IRA. Bold policies for phasing out internal combustion engines and gas-fired central heating are facing significant resistance and the Commission will need to hold its ground. The international impact of Europe's proposed CBAM requires dialogue, and the International Climate Club, originally proposed by Germany and now announced by the G7, is a promising idea.

The UK

The UK contributes just over 1% of global CO_2 emissions although, because the industrial revolution began in the UK, its share of cumulative emissions since 1750 is significantly higher, at around 5%. As a "post industrial" society with a relatively small share of heavy industry in its economy, the UK has a level of emissions per person and per unit of GDP that is less than two thirds of the average for developed nations.[113]

Between 1990 and 2020, the UK reduced its CO_2 emissions by nearly 50%. On a "consumption" basis, that is to say, accounting for the emissions embedded in imports and exports, the figure is a somewhat less impressive 30%.

The UK's big success has been to reduce, and almost eliminate, the generation of electricity from coal and replace it partly with gas but now, to an increasing extent, with renewables, especially offshore wind. The UK closed its historic deep mining coal industry in the 1970s and 1980s, as it had become uneconomic. At the time, this was a tough political decision which caused extensive social unrest. With no mining jobs at stake, the more recent closure of the coal power stations, running on imported coal, was much less controversial and politically much easier.

Following Denmark's lead, the UK pioneered the development of offshore wind through a series of auctions in which the government guaranteed the price of the electricity generated. At first, the price required to attract investment was high compared to the cost of gas-powered electricity, but more recently, as the industry has built up its capacity and the size of individual wind generators has increased, the price came down to well below the day ahead wholesale price of electricity although it has rebounded somewhat since. This has been a big success for the UK and it has also contributed to the global effort to drive down the cost of energy transition.

As a result of phasing out coal and investing in offshore wind, the UK has reduced its emissions from power generation by 66% between 1990 and 2022, a massive achievement. However, wind energy is variable and not always available at times of high electricity demand. As the share of wind energy increases, so will the need for back-up in the form of electricity storage, demand side flexibility, nuclear power, and possibly coal or gas stations with captured emissions.

The UK has been somewhat less successful in reducing emissions from transport, industry, and buildings, which are the other main sectors. Transport emissions have come down only by 11% between 1990 and 2022, making transport now the biggest source. The government's main climate policies for transport have focused on the introduction of electric vehicles. Government policies for subsidising electric vehicles have been phased out as uptake has increased, but there is growing investment in charging points. The government had announced that new petrol or diesel cars would be banned from 2030, but has now advanced this to 2035. There is already, in 2023, a certain amount of push-back against this policy in the media and the industry. Attracting the necessary investment in electric cars, and especially in batteries, is a serious challenge. Hopefully, the government will stick to its guns.

Business emissions have come down by 44% between 1990 and 2022, partly as a result of changes in the structure of the UK economy but also as a result of levies on business emissions, including the UK's ETS, which continues, post Brexit, to mirror the European scheme. However, the technologies needed to decarbonise heavy industries, such as steel, aluminium, or cement, have not yet been commercialised at reasonable cost. It looks as though large investment will be needed in carbon capture and storage (CCS), hydrogen, and possibly high-temperature nuclear power. That is a challenge for the future.

Residential emissions, mainly due to gas central heating, accounted for 17% of the UK's CO_2 emissions in 2022. They had declined by 17% since 1990, mainly thanks to the government's successful drive for the adoption of more efficient condensing boilers.[114] The government has said it will ban gas central heating in new homes from 2025. As discussed in Chapter 2 on technology above, heat pumps are already a viable option for new homes that can be designed with levels of insulation and appropriate heating systems, but are less suitable for existing homes. The UK has a high proportion of older homes, much loved by the public, which are only being replaced at the rate of about 1% p.a. Government efforts to persuade the public to improve their insulation have had limited success. For the longer term the government has a proposal to ban new gas boiler installations in existing homes from 2035.

The government is undecided whether heat pumps or hydrogen, or some combination, should be the longer-term solution for low-carbon home and business heating. The government hopes that banning gas heating for new buildings will create a mass market for heat pumps that will drive down costs. However, as mentioned above, local trials of hydrogen heating have faced public resistance. At some point, householders will have to make a change that will be inconvenient and costly. Nobody is preparing the public for that. As already mentioned, the government says that its strategy is focused on "reducing bills and improving comfort".[115]

The UK's energy transition strategy is constrained by the limitations of government finance. Major additional spending programmes, firstly to sustain employment during the COVID-19 epidemic and then to shield consumers from the spike in gas prices during 2021 and 2022, have drained the coffers. Government debt is now approximately equal to GDP, a historically high level which the government is struggling to stabilise and eventually reduce. There have been cuts in subsidies for electric vehicles, in support of energy efficiency in buildings, and, as discussed below, in overseas development aid. The government is seeking international finance for its programme of nuclear power.

In 2008, the government established the Climate Change Committee (CCC) as a new statutory body with the aim of overseeing the government's progress towards meeting climate objectives. The CCC sets five-year emissions "budgets" which, once accepted, the government has a legal obligation to meet. It also publishes regular appraisals of progress and makes policy recommendations. The verdict of the CCC's 2022 Progress Report is that, "Despite important achievements on renewable energy and electric vehicles, the government is failing in much of its implementation". The CCC has also concluded that, "The government has made a clear choice to rely heavily on technology with much less focus on efficiency [and] improvements in demand management across the economy ... this could lead the UK down a more expensive path to net zero with a higher risk of failure on energy security".[116]

In 2022, a group of environmental NGOs successfully sued the UK government on the grounds that its policies were not adequate to reduce emissions in line with the budgets set out by the CCC, forcing the government to review its strategy. Having an independent body with legal powers and the ability to review and assess the government's climate policies has undoubtedly added to the pressure on the government to adopt a credible strategy. We badly need similar international rigour to assess the policies of governments around the world for achieving their net zero targets. It is too much to expect that there could be a global body with quite the powers of the CCC. The options for strengthening world governance for climate mitigation are discussed in Chapter 6.

The UK's investment in advanced technologies, such as CCS and hydrogen, has so far been relatively modest. On CCS in particular, the UK has an unhappy story of repeated initiatives being pulled for lack of finance, dashing the proposals that industry had been invited to put forward.

In recent years, the UK has spent 0.7% of the GDP on overseas development aid, the target set by the UN. However, in 2021, the government decided to "temporarily" reduce this to 0.5%, citing financial strains. It was an unfortunate step given the needs of the developing world for support in their low-carbon transition, a topic that is discussed in depth in Chapter 5. But £11 billion plus p.a. is still a substantial contribution.

The government has committed to spend £11.6 billion on International Climate Finance between the years 2021/2002 and 2022/2023, being the UK's contribution towards the $100 billion p.a. by 2020 promised by the developed nations at the Copenhagen Climate Summit in 2008. According to an October 2021 study by the World Resources Institute, the UK was not quite contributing its fair share of the promised $100 billion although it was not far off.

In important respects, the UK is a leader in climate transition. But there are significant areas where it has not yet faced up to the challenge of net zero. This partly reflects a lack of finance to bring forward key technologies for the future and partly an unwillingness to face the public with the need to change consumption patterns. The CCC was an excellent initiative which other nations might be encouraged to follow. The UK has a respectable record on international development and climate aid which has also, in recent years, been limited by financial constraints. As with other developed nations, however, this still does not measure up to the future needs of the developing world. The reduction in development aid from 0.7% of GDP to 0.5% was intended to be temporary and it is to be hoped that this can be reversed in the next few years.

India

India has large coal reserves and, as with China, its economy is largely coal-driven. 72% of India's electricity is coal-powered and 44% of its total energy supply.

India contributes 6.7% of global CO_2 emissions. However, its economy is growing rapidly. Electricity demand nearly tripled between 2000 and 2020.[117] In the IEA's Stated Policies Scenario, nearly a quarter of the global increase in energy demand in the next two decades will be in India and by 2030, India will be on the point of taking over from the US as the world's second biggest emitter, only behind China.

All this reflects India's huge population. India has just, in 2023, overtaken China as the most populous nation on earth. So although India's total emissions are large, emissions per head are less than half the global average and about one fifth of the average for developed OECD member countries.[118]

India has eight national missions in its climate strategy: solar, energy efficiency, sustainable habitat, water, Himalayan eco-system, green India, sustainable agriculture, and strategic knowledge.

The Indian government has made major climate commitments, most recently set out in Prime Minister Modi's address to the Glasgow Climate Summit.[119] These included deriving 50% of energy from renewables by 2030, reducing carbon intensity by more than 45% by 2030, and achieving net zero by 2070. These aims are impressive. However, Prime Minister Modi has said that this is conditional on India receiving $1 trillion in international climate finance. These aims also demonstrate how far we are from achieving climate objectives bearing in mind that, according to the IEA, we need to achieve global net zero by around 2050 to contain global warming to 1.5°C. In common with most other developing countries, India has avoided setting any absolute limit on its future emissions prior to its net zero target, no doubt in order to avoid putting a straightjacket on economic growth.

For India, solar power has been a big success. It is economically competitive and has attracted major international investment. Much of India's rapid growth in electricity demand is for air conditioning and this demand fits sufficiently closely with the hours of sunlight that battery storage can bridge the difference. Today, India has a surplus of coal fired generating capacity, but in some regions, there are frequent blackouts because of shortages of coal. Solar power can help to conserve coal supplies. Solar power can also, eventually, help to solve the weaknesses in India's electricity distribution system. Prime Minister Modi is the founder and supporter of the International Solar Alliance. According to the IEA, India is "on the cusp of a solar power revolution".

Although a lot of private and international investment has gone into India's solar boom, its success is very much the result of government action. Revenues from solar power are guaranteed by the government or government agencies with the price set by auction. And the government has intervened in other ways to ensure the availability of land and necessary infrastructure. Prices of solar power in India today have fallen to a small fraction of their level only a few years ago.

It is not surprising that, along with China, India bridled at the proposal, in the draft Glasgow communique, to "phase out coal". Hundreds of millions of people in India as well as China have, in recent decades, been lifted from extreme poverty, on the back of a rapid increase in coal power. These countries cannot give that up in any short period without a loss of energy security, especially as both have limited access to gas.

India is pursuing a wide range of progressive low-carbon energy policies.[120] These include policies for switching to efficient LED lighting, promotion of relatively clean compressed gas powered vehicles, regulation of commercial buildings, standards for the efficiency of cars and support for electric vehicles. India has a major government initiative, known as Perform, Achieve and Trade (PAT), in which major industries are set efficiency targets and have the opportunity to trade credits if they exceed them. Peak electricity demand in much of India is for cooling and the government has a "Cooling Action Plan" for the regulation of buildings and cooling appliances.

India achieved near-universal household access to electricity in 2019, undoubtedly a major achievement. However, there is a chronic shortage of reliable power and many regions suffer frequent outages. This is in part a result of the financial weakness of the electricity distribution industry. The distribution companies suffer from regulated prices that do not always cover costs. An additional problem is the non-payment of bills by customers, including municipalities. They have had to be bailed out by the government repeatedly.

India is at an earlier stage in industrial development than China, and there are already signs that India will not follow the same, ultra carbon-intensive pathway. The pathway that India does choose will be critical for the global climate. The growth of solar energy in India is impressive and certainly an encouraging sign. But it remains to be seen how soon India can start to reduce, significantly, its dependence on coal and how India meets the energy needs of its rapidly growing cities, transport infrastructure, and increasingly affluent consumers. We cannot afford to ignore India's call for international climate investment. Most recently, in May 2023, India has revised its draft energy policy to say that no more coal power stations are expected to be needed beyond approximately 32 GW of capacity already under construction. That would be a major step in the global climate effort. The super-tanker of global energy is beginning to turn, if not yet fast enough.

Massive national and international finance will be required to finance the transformation of the Indian power system, but this is held back by the high cost of capital. The required return on equity, according to the IEA,[121] has recently been in the range of 15–20% p.a., reflecting a high level of perceived risk. This is partly due to the relatively undeveloped state of India's capital markets. It is also due to a combination of the weak finances of the distribution companies, uncertainty over government regulation, and currency risk, although the rupee has been fairly stable in recent years. The yield on Indian government 10-year bonds is about 7%, relatively low for a developing economy but still significantly higher than for bonds of developed nations. India's credit rating with S&P Global Ratings is BBB, which counts as a low level investment grade.

India has always said that its emissions targets are conditional on receiving extensive international financial aid, and it does indeed seem clear that a massive infusion of international finance will be required to set India on a credible low-carbon pathway. However, India has been relatively successful in attracting private capital to its rapidly growing solar power sector and hopefully, it will be possible to build on that.

India can be a leader of other developing nations at a similar stage of industrialisation as well as being a champion of the interests of developing countries in the climate negotiations in the search for climate justice.

South Africa

South Africa is responsible for only just over 1% of global CO_2 emissions although, because of its heavy reliance on coal, its emissions per GDP are more than twice the global average. South Africa illustrates some of the difficulties that investors face in financing the energy transitions of developing countries.

South Africa has proposed a range of progressive low-carbon policies, including buildings' efficiency regulation and the regulation of biofuels for transport, and is in the process of implementing a carbon tax. South Africa has committed to an absolute level of greenhouse gas emissions in 2030 of 18–31% below 2010 levels.[122] At the Glasgow Summit South Africa brought forward the date when its emissions will peak from 2035 to 2025. But the government said that it will need $8 billion p.a. of international finance, more than three times the current level, to achieve this.

South Africa's government has been plagued by corruption and administrative inefficiency. A particular problem in moving away from coal, which is mined domestically, is the very high level of unemployment. Replacements have to be found for lost jobs in the coal industry. Investment in renewables can create new jobs, but not necessarily in the right place.

The dominant energy challenge in South Africa today is the shortage of electric power.[123] The monopoly state-owned integrated power company Eskom is responsible for generation, transmission, and distribution. Eskom has suffered chronic financial difficulties as a result of internal corruption, price regulation that does not reflect generation costs, and non-payment of bills by municipalities. There has been insufficient new capacity and, most significantly, a failure to maintain existing plant leading to poor availability. South Africa has suffered severe electric blackouts in recent years and the government has had to bail Eskom out repeatedly. The problem goes beyond South Africa itself because South Africa also provides power to neighbouring countries in Sub-Saharan Africa.

The government's 1998 White Paper contained progressive policies for restructuring and liberalising the electricity supply industry. Eskom was to be "unbundled" and separate new entities were to be created for generation, transmission, and distribution. A competitive market in electricity was to be created, and Independent Power Producers (IPPs) were to have equal access to the system. International financial institutions have been pressing for these changes.

Progress has been stalled for 20 years as vested interests and administrative infighting have resisted change. The government has undertaken a series of auctions for renewable capacity but these have been slowed by the rigidities of the system. Perhaps the necessary reforms are about to take off now.

South Africa has very promising renewables potential, and investment in renewables is undoubtedly the way forward for the medium and longer term. However, the immediate need to meet today's crisis of electricity supply, is for the maintenance of existing coal power stations to make them more reliable. International partners should support that as part of a medium- and longer-term low-carbon strategy.

Most recently, at a meeting with donor countries, South Africa has sought around $27 billion in concessionary international finance to expand its transmission grid, strengthen its distribution network, and expedite diversification from coal.

South Africa presents a challenge for the international donor community. Now that the costs have come down so sharply, investment in renewables should be profitable. But there are major barriers. Financing an electricity generation project generally requires a reliable stream of future income from power sales, sufficient to pay the interest on the debt. There has to be a long-term contract with a "counterparty" with a well-defined price. In South Africa, it may be difficult to find a sufficiently reliable counterparty. Eskom itself is financially troubled and the payments track record of municipalities has been mixed. Successful unbundling and liberalisation of the power industry could open more avenues for electricity supply and, therefore, increase the range of possible counterparties.

Probably the most secure option today, if available, would be a government "sovereign guarantee". However, the government itself is financially pressed. Its credit rating with rating agency S&P Global Ratings is BB- which is below the investment grade required by big insurance companies and pension funds and implies significant risk. The South African government's 10-year bond yields interest of around 10% p.a. That is moderate compared to the bonds of other developing countries, but it is still high compared to most Western government bonds traded in the range of 2–5% (although all somewhat volatile in August 2023). This also implies a significant perception of risk. Compared to many developing country currencies, the Rand has been relatively stable in recent years, declining in value from about 8 US cents in 2018 to 6 US cents today, but that also is part of the risk that international investors take.

For all these reasons, it will be difficult to attract large-scale international commercial investment in the South African energy transition. Part of the solution is to work with the South African government to help it to reform the power system so that the country's energy institutions are financially sound.

That is being attempted now. In November 2021, the governments of France, Germany, the US, and the EU announced an "International Just Energy Transition Partnership" with the government of South Africa to "support South Africa's decarbonisation effort" and specifically the move away from coal. The partnership is to mobilise $8.5 billion over 3–5 years. This will include multilateral and bilateral grants, concessional loans, guarantees, and private investments. The aim is to accelerate decarbonisation through the early closure of coal power stations. The finance will "protect vulnerable individuals and communities" and support the reform of the electricity sector. We must hope that all this can be achieved. The obstacles lie deep.

Even if the donor nations are willing to fund the South African energy transition on a concessionary basis, reform of the power sector may be needed for that money to be used effectively. The ability to attract commercial finance is an acid test of the soundness of energy institutions.

One approach to this is creative finance, especially the "blending" of fully commercial finance with concessionary development finance to reduce the commercial risks to acceptable levels. That is something that we can expect to see on a larger scale. Another is the provision of total or partial guarantees.

Commercial finance will be needed, along with concessionary development finance, to achieve the necessary energy transition in the developing world. It would be naïve to think otherwise. Opening this door will be vital for the climate effort, and the question of how to achieve it is considered at length in the next chapter.

Indonesia

Indonesia has a population of 270 million, making it the fourth most populous nation in the world. Its economy has been growing rapidly and Indonesia is now classified by the World Bank as an upper middle income country. A major achievement in the energy sector is that access to electricity has improved from 53% in 2000 to 100% today. Total CO_2 emissions are nearly 600 million tonnes p.a., representing about 1.7% of the global total. Indonesia enjoys an investment grade credit rating of BBB with S&P.

Over the coming three decades, the country's population is expected to rise to 335 million people, the economy to more than triple in size, and primary energy supply also to triple. The potential impact on global emissions is immense.

Indonesia is rich in coal. Its generating capacity grew approximately three fold between 2009 and 2020. As a result, the national fleet of coal power stations is relatively young, with an average age of about 10 years. Today, 62% of Indonesia's electric power is coal-fired. The remainder is mainly gas and hydro. There is some geothermal and bio power, but very little wind or solar power today. Indonesia has recently overtaken Australia to become the largest coal exporter in the world.

Indonesia has announced policies for a carbon tax on coal power and a carbon trading mechanism and has conducted auctions for renewable energy. But the impact has been fairly limited thus far.

The government has set a target of net zero by 2060, "or sooner with international support" and a 29% reduction in greenhouse gas emissions "through our own efforts" by 2030 or 41% "with international support". The intention is to end the building of new coal power stations beyond those already in the pipeline. However, there are up to 35 Gigawatts of capacity in this pipeline, which is about half of Indonesia's total generating capacity today.

Both the International Renewable Energy Agency (IRENA)[124] and the International Energy Agency (IEA)[125] have studied Indonesia's pathway to low-carbon energy transition with the government. In IRENA's business as usual case based on "current and planned policies", emissions increase by at least 80% by 2050. In their sustainable case, which achieves much reduced emissions, two-thirds of Indonesia's energy comes from renewables in 2060, as compared to 14% today. This case requires $332 billion of investment in renewables, electric vehicles, and associated infrastructure by 2030. In the longer term, it requires up to $2.4 trillion of cumulative investment by 2050, which is about double the investment in the energy sector in the business as usual case. Because of the savings in fossil fuel, IRENA estimates that the low-carbon case is less costly overall.

The IEA's study also envisages a rapid switch to renewables, but it also emphasises the importance of improving energy efficiency, especially for air conditioning.

According to the OECD, Indonesia received $2.7 billion of development aid from OECD countries in 2021, mainly from the US, Japan, and Germany, and mostly in areas, such as "health, social infrastructure, economic infrastructure, humanitarian aid".[126]

Indonesia is a prime recipient of Belt and Road investment, mainly from China's development bank. Much of this has been for roads and railways, but it has also included coal fired power plants and hydro power plants. Total Chinese investment in Indonesia was running at over $8 billion p.a. in 2020. As already mentioned, China has said that it will not finance any more coal fired plant overseas.

In November 2022, the US, Japan, and partners announced that they would mobilise $20 billion of public and private finance to help Indonesia shut coal power plants. Indonesia agreed to bring forward the date when its energy emissions will peak by 7 years to 2030 and that a third of its electric power will be from renewables by 2030. Major banks, including Citibank, Deutsche Bank, HSBC, and Standard Chartered, are expected to contribute to finance.[127] The deal has been criticised by some because Indonesia will not call a halt to planned new coal power stations.

Indonesia is a test case. Hugely dependent on coal today, Indonesia has massive renewables potential. The transition has barely begun. An international effort has mobilised to accelerate it. But moving away from coal will probably be a rather slow process.

Nigeria

Nigeria is not a big part of the global climate problem today.[128] Emissions per head are about 5% of the global average and total emissions contribute about one-half of 1% to the global total. Nigeria has a large and rapidly growing population of 200 million. The country desperately needs economic development. GDP per capita is only about $2,000 p.a. and 40% of the population lives in poverty. Only 60% have access to electricity and 10% have access to clean cooking. Nigeria has electricity generating capacity of around 12 Gigawatts, mainly gas fuelled, but less than half of this is usually available due to gas shortages, "a decrepit grid network, high losses in transmission and distribution, and debt crises in the industry".[129] Diesel-powered backup generators abound.

Nigeria is ranked 154 out of 180 countries in the Corruption Perceptions Index published by Transparency International. Inflation is over 20% p.a. and the currency has depreciated. S&Ps credit rating for Nigeria is B-, well below investment grade with a negative outlook.

Nigeria has the largest oil and gas reserves in Sub-Saharan Africa, and oil and gas production contributes nearly 80% of government revenues. Nigeria is Africa's largest oil producer. Nigeria's gas potential is considered to be even greater. Nigeria also has huge potential for renewables, including solar, hydro, geothermal, biomass, and wind. How these resources are used to achieve economic progress will be enormously important for the welfare of Nigerians and also for the climate.

Today, 80% of Nigeria's electric power is from gas and most of the rest from oil. The government's Renewable Energy Master Plan is for 2,000 MW of small hydro, 500 MW of solar PV, 400 MW of biomass, and 40 MW of wind, all by 2025. These are fairly modest ambitions. To put them in perspective, Nigeria has about 12,000 MW of generating capacity today. Nigeria has to flare much of its natural gas, produced in association with oil, for want of infrastructure to make use of it.

The World Bank is not optimistic about Nigeria's immediate prospects, "Oil price booms have previously supported the Nigerian economy but this has not been the case since 2021 … declining oil production and the mounting costs of petrol subsidies have prevented Nigeria from reaping the benefits of higher oil prices". The reasons given for declining oil production include security challenges, inadequate investments, and the failure of the Nigerian National Petroleum Company to pay the government's share in joint ventures.

The World Bank continues that, "while Nigeria has made some progress in socio-economic terms in recent years, its human capital development ranked only 150 of 157 countries in the World Bank's 2020 Human Capital Index. The country continues to face massive development challenges, including the need to reduce the dependence on oil for exports and revenues, diversify its foreign exchange sources, close the infrastructure gap, build strong and effective institutions, as well as address governance issues and strengthen public financial management systems".[130]

The Nigerian government has committed to net zero by 2060. A Power Sector Reform Act of 2005 provided for the unbundling and privatisation of Nigeria's power industry. However implementation has been bedevilled by conflicts of interest and has not led to the creation of strong and well financed institutions capable of attracting international investment. The government now claims to have achieved cost reflective electricity tariffs and a 75% increase in collections. So, hopefully, there is progress towards a stronger financial base.

In 2021, shortly after announcing its net zero target, the government issued its Energy Transition Plan, prepared in partnership with The Rockefeller Foundation and other green NGOs. Gas is recognised as an important transition fuel, but there is minimal investment in the "declining" oil sector. The medium- and longer-term strategy is for massive investment in renewables, especially utility-scale solar, and electricity storage. There is also significant investment in electricity micro-grids. A first step, to be achieved by 2025, is to "secure agreement to local manufacturing and assembly of key technologies".

Following the announcement of this plan, Nigeria has launched an international appeal for a $10 billion support package.

In recent years, Nigeria has been receiving between $2 and $3 billion p.a. in development aid, directly or indirectly, from the OECD countries.[131] The precise level of Chinese investment is difficult to assess, but according to the Debt Management Office of Nigeria, its total debt to China was $3.12 billion and this constituted 4% of Nigeria's total public debt.

There is a significant difference in the development programmes supported by China and the West. Almost all of China's loans were tied to major road, rail, or airport construction projects carried out by Chinese companies. Western aid supported diverse aspects of the government's development plans. For instance, in December 2020, the World Bank announced a wide-ranging $1.4 billion financial package of support. The areas included education, healthcare, and projects for "strengthening the foundations of the public sector", "unlocking private investment", and "digital infrastructure".

Attracting private finance to support the energy transition in Nigeria will require confidence-building measures. These may include guarantees covering currency and other risks. International development banks may lead, developing projects and contributing a share of risk capital. They will also need to support projects for strengthening Nigeria's energy sector institutions. An Oxford University study[132] suggests that Nigeria's own Bank of Industry, if suitably strengthened, could have an important role. Part of the problem has been that development aid has not been coordinated and the study suggests that, "an optimal strategy with higher potential multiplier effects would require donors to coordinate their financial resources and technical assistance to incentivise large scale investments in renewable technology".

In June 2023, the newly elected President Bola Tinubu announced the abandonment of a long-held national policy of pegging the Nigerian currency, the Naira, to an official rate accessible only to insiders. Hopefully, this will mark the start of a new era in which Nigeria becomes more accessible to international investment.[133]

In the short term, Nigeria is desperately dependent on its oil and gas production. It seems unfair for relatively rich developed nations in the West, themselves still producing and consuming oil and gas, to attempt to restrict investment in this vital sector. The government of Nigeria has agreed that the future is with renewables, but it is much more difficult to attract investment in this sector and Nigeria is calling for international aid. The weakness of Nigeria's institutions, its high level of indebtedness, and the pervading corruption all make it difficult for donors to invest effectively and to attract private capital. But we have to try. Efforts need to concentrate on supporting and reforming Nigeria's energy sector institutions and on options for de-risking private sector investment.

Conclusion

Government policy is an essential element in the climate equation. The need for government regulatory action is the fourth key energy policy. All major governments have extensive policies in place or in preparation. But these are far from sufficient for meeting the net zero challenge. The US has made generous financial provisions, but the Federal government is not regulating sufficiently to end America's love affair with oil or, to a lesser degree, coal. The EU has a set of powerful regulations in place but some of these are being challenged and it is not yet clear to what extent it will follow the US example of major subsidies for clean energy technologies. China still struggles to reduce dependence on coal while maintaining rapid economic growth and energy security. India, South Africa, Nigeria, and Indonesia will require massive international finance to achieve low-carbon economic development. This represents a huge challenge to the community of developed nations and the international financial institutions. The challenges of financing low-carbon transition in the developing world are discussed further in the following chapter.

Chapter 5

International Relations: Cooperation in a House Divided

Key Policy No. 5.

The effort to limit climate change has profound geopolitical implications. We see this in the struggle for leadership in key technologies and for access to vital materials, in the climate negotiations themselves, and in the emerging threat of climate nationalism. At the heart of this is Key Climate Policy No. 5, the need to support the developing world, because without low-carbon transition in the developing world the climate cause is lost. We also have to find a way to cooperate with China. China is not only the largest emitter, but also a leader in climate technology. China also has considerable influence in the developing world and is the largest investor in developing countries. For all these reasons, cooperation with China is essential to the achievement of climate goals.

Introduction

Climate mitigation has to be a global effort for the simple reason that we all share one planet. International cooperation is of the essence. There has to be a fair division of effort between the nations. The rich nations have to provide support for the poorer developing nations. The international impacts of national climate policies have to be managed. Cooperation is needed to share implementation plans, policies, and technologies. Governments have to learn from each other and demonstrate not only that they have ambitious targets for energy transition but also that they have credible implementation strategies. All this has to be achieved in a world with weak global governance and that is full of divisions and tensions.

This chapter reviews international relations for achieving energy transition. It considers the dangers of climate nationalism and competition for access to strategic materials, before focusing on relations between the rich and poor nations and then the crucial relationship between China and the West.

Climate Nationalism

One of the threats to global progress on climate change is that inward-looking national climate policies may undermine international trust. Positive domestic climate policies may be counter-productive if they undermine trust in developing countries and weaken the international co-operation that is at the heart of the global climate effort.

Much of President Biden's Inflation Reduction Act takes the form of subsidies for the deployment of low-carbon technology on the condition that it is manufactured in the US. This is a clear breach of World Trade Organization rules. It can inhibit trade in low-carbon products and promote the migration of green manufacturing industries from US trading partners to the US. Not surprisingly, this is causing protests, not only in the EU but also in the developing world.

The EU has been negotiating with the US to try to gain exemptions for EU industry. But in a joint paper of December 2022, the French and German economic ministers argued that if these talks fail, the EU should relax its internal rules on state aid to enable EU national governments to match the US subsidies.[134]

While the support for green industries in the IRA is welcome, the "made in America" restrictions will prevent beneficiaries from accessing the cheapest sources of supply, raise the price of green components, and, therefore, moderate the benefit to the environment. They will antagonise exporting nations and raise the risk of eroding international trust in the transition process. It is understandable that the US wishes to limit its dependence on China for strategic materials and products, but the restrictions in the IRA go much further than that.

The emergence of Carbon Border Adjustment Mechanism (CBAM) also threatens trade between developed and developing nations.

For the purposes of the Climate Treaty, national emissions are measured on a "production" basis. In other words, they cover what is actually emitted in the country concerned. This ignores the fact that products whose manufacture gave rise to emissions may be traded. For some countries, it makes quite a significant difference if emissions are accounted for on a "consumption" basis, adding emissions embodied in imports, and subtracting those in exports. China's emissions on a consumption basis are about 10% less than on a production basis.[135] According to an OECD study, in 2015 OECD countries imported goods with embodied emissions of nearly 3 Gt of CO_2 equivalent and exported embodied emissions of about 1 Gt of CO_2 equivalent. UK greenhouse gas emissions in 2021 were 347 m tonnes of CO_2 equivalent on a production basis, but 513 m tonnes of CO_2 equivalent on a consumption basis,[136] a significant difference.

There is a practical reason why emissions embodied in imports and exports are ignored under the Climate Treaty. Governments have control over the emissions emitted internally, but they have, at least so far, no control over the emissions from overseas factories. Hitherto neither the exporting nor the importing countries have wanted to change that. The importers have welcomed access to cheap goods with no carbon charge and the exporters have no wish to have foreign countries interfering in their industrial production, putting up costs, and possibly inhibiting economic growth and job creation. However, this balance is changing as the developing countries tighten the environmental screws on their domestic industries. These industries are complaining, increasingly, about "unfair" competition with imports from less regulated nations.

Both the US and the EU are considering CBAMs, in other words, taxes on the carbon content of imported goods. The argument is that these border taxes are needed to create a level playing field and to encourage exporting nations to impose their own carbon taxes. There would be exemptions for nations that could show that they had comparable carbon regimes.

Developing nations have a different point of view. They are relying on the growth of exports to the developed world to spur economic development. That is how the Chinese economic miracle took off. The Climate Treaty makes it clear that it is for the developed nations to lead in the adoption of climate policies, a principle embodied in the phrase, "common but differentiated responsibilities". From the perspective of developing nations, the adoption of border adjustments seems like a threat to their economic progress and an attempt to force then to move in parallel with richer developed nations.

At the Sharm El-Sheikh Climate Summit, the BASIC group consisting of Brazil, South Africa, India, and China, protested that, "Unilateral measures and discriminatory practices, such as carbon border taxes, that could result in market distortion and aggravate the trust deficit among Parties [to the UNFCCC], must be avoided".[137]

In general terms it is reasonable to fear the growth of climate nationalism. In other words, measures that support domestic low-carbon transformation, but which have negative international impacts and which may, as the BASIC nations have pointed out, contribute to the trust deficit. Such measures can be expected to have a greater impact as the low-carbon transformation deepens.

Governments need to consider the impacts of domestic measures that they take on the global transition. The only solution to the problem of climate nationalism is better dialogue. The proposal of several German government departments, already mentioned in Chapter 3, and now implemented by the G7, for "International Climate Clubs" is a possible way of dealing with this. In other words, developed nations could agree to a package of measures with developing nations. If they included CBAMs, they would also include financial help to enable developing countries to develop their own low-carbon measures and qualify for complete or partial exemption. These arrangements could be negotiated bilaterally. They could also be negotiated through a strengthened centre for global climate cooperation, such as is proposed later in Chapter 6. However, for such a negotiation to be at all realistic, the developed nations would have to find ways to substantially enhance the flow of funds for green investment in the developing world, a major topic later in this chapter.

Strategic Energy Materials

We have become used to a world in which oil and gas security are among the major issues of international relations. That isn't going to change soon.

The war in Ukraine and the scramble for energy supplies have reminded us of that. Oil is going to play a substantial part in world energy supply for at least another decade and possibly well beyond that. Security of energy supply will still be vital. But eventually, as the climate effort continues, we will become less dependent on oil and, probably rather later, also gas.

One might expect that as oil demand eventually declines, and production from higher-cost oilfields is no longer needed, prices will move closer to those of the lowest-cost fields, possibly in the range of \$10–20 per billion, or even below. However, most of these fields belong to OPEC countries, so they will dominate the market. With sufficient discipline, OPEC may retain some ability to support prices for several decades to come. As oil and gas prices do eventually decline, importing country governments will see an opportunity to increase the tax on these fuels without popular outcry. The revenues may be available to support energy transition. In the absence of such taxes, low oil and gas prices could undermine the economic incentives for low-carbon investment.

When world oil prices collapse, the countries most dependent on oil exports may face an economic crisis. Algeria, Venezuela, Nigeria, Saudi Arabia, and perhaps even Russia, are prime candidates. We may not have much sympathy with governments that have lived for many decades on oil rents extracted from the West. But failed states cast a long shadow of misery and violence. We should do what we can to help these countries to diversify their economies. Saudi Arabia has a major national project to diversify its economy beyond oil, as has the UAE which hosted COP 28. They could become leading sources of low-carbon hydrogen based on solar PV or possibly gas with stored emissions. Conversion of oil and gas exporting nations into low-carbon hydrogen or electricity investors and exporters could make a valuable contribution to the low-carbon transition.

We cannot assume that the eventual run-down of oil production will relieve geopolitical tensions over energy materials and supplies. As the old dependency on oil declines, new dependencies on materials that are essential for the electric age will arise.

Technical developments may or may not ease the need for some of these materials. More intensive world-wide exploration may yield new and increased sources of supply. International trade in hydrogen and electricity may also become important.

High on the list of the West's geopolitical concerns is the dominance of China in the manufacture of renewable energy equipment, and of electric batteries, and in the extraction and production of key materials. Rare earths and lithium are essential for a wide range of advanced technologies, including batteries and renewable power. However, they are not especially rare. It is the extraction and processing that is concentrated in China, not the reserves. There was a crisis in 2011, as China reduced its export quotas and prices spiked in the expectation of rapidly increasing demand. But this proved short-lived as mines opened up in the US and Australia and manufacturers found technical options that somewhat reduced the need for these materials.[138]

The experience of 2011 shows that China may be willing to use strategic materials as a political lever. China is certainly capable of producing a major short-term supply crisis. But this would be at the expense of provoking a rapid build-up of alternative production and a loss of markets for the longer term. Most probably, Chinese authorities realised this when they backed down on their threats. Nevertheless, China still has a stranglehold on supply in the shorter term. It is certainly prudent for Western governments to invest to diversify their supply options. There is a lesson to be learnt from the war in Ukraine and Europe's difficulty in weaning itself from Russian gas in a short period. Through the IRA, the US is responding vigorously to this threat by super-charging its own key industries and Europe is aiming to follow suit.

Large-scale international trade in electricity would create dependencies in some respects even more acute than dependence on oil imports. For instance, there is a proposal for large-scale export of electricity generated from solar PV in North Africa to Europe. If this became a major source of supply, serious questions of security would arise. What if supplies were suddenly cut off due to a political change in the exporting nation?

The International Energy Agency (IEA) was founded to manage the dependency of the West on imported oil. One could imagine a regime in which importers of critical climate-related materials or of electricity or hydrogen committed themselves to mutual support in the event of a crisis of supply. The case for expanding the IEA's role is discussed in Chapter 6.

The growing risk of climate nationalism in the form of inward-looking climate policies calls for the negotiation of more comprehensive relations between developed and developing nations on climate change, and the level of support will inevitably be part of the equation. However, Western governments are right to protect themselves from the strategic risks posed by China's near monopoly of key materials and products.

Relations Between Rich and Poor Nations

The rich nations have a moral obligation to support the poor nations, and it is also in their interests to do so. The need to support developing nations is the fifth key energy policy listed at the start of this book.

The developed nations have a heavy responsibility. Historically, and in terms of emissions per head, the West is by far the biggest polluter. Since 1750, the cumulative energy related emissions of the US and the UK have each reached more than a thousand tonnes of CO_2 per person,[139] whereas China has emitted just over 150 tonnes and India less than 40 tonnes per person. The whole of Africa, with 17% of the world's population, contributes just 4% of current emissions and a much smaller share of accumulated emissions. Yet Africa, especially Sub-Saharan Africa, which already suffers from high temperatures and drought, is one of the regions most vulnerable to climate change. Small island states, whose very existence is threatened by rising sea levels, are in a similar position.

One can debate at large the overall impact of the Industrial Revolution, spreading from the West, on the developing world. It's a big subject. Plainly, there have been major benefits. However, one consequence is that the developed countries are primarily responsible for the greenhouse gas emissions already in the atmosphere which now have grave consequences, especially for the developing countries which are least able to protect themselves. The developed countries have a heavy moral duty to take the lead in emissions reduction, and to help developing countries now beginning their own industrial revolutions to follow a different path. That includes, but is not limited to, delivering on the promises made in the Climate Treaty and subsequent climate agreements. As described in Chapter 1, at the 2022 Climate Summit, the developed nations also agreed to set up a fund to compensate developing countries for loss and damage.

Governments of developed countries also have to consider the impact of their own domestic policies for climate transition on the developing world. As discussed above, "climate nationalism" runs the risk of impeding the ability of developing countries to achieve low-carbon growth.

It is also strongly in the national interests of developed countries to provide support. Most emissions today, and all the growth in emissions, are in the developing world. They have most of the world's population. Regions such as India and Sub-Saharan Africa are on the cusp of industrial revolutions that can raise the living standards of billions of people but which will also require prodigious quantities of energy. The average Indian today uses only 17% as much energy as people living in the West, but that is set to change, with momentous consequences for world energy and for the climate. The West cannot solve the climate problem on its own. The biggest challenge is in the developing world. Unless the developing nations can be assisted to follow a low-carbon path, the efforts to reduce emissions in the West will be in vain. To paraphrase the 17th century English poet John Donne, "No nation is an island unto itself, we are a part of the main". The "breakdown of food systems and rural livelihoods" seen by the IPCC as one of the main risks would have international consequences. "Send not to know for whom the bell of climate change tolls. It tolls for thee".

Looking at developing countries as a whole, in most cases, their reductions to 2030 are either expressed in terms of the emissions intensity of GDP, or they are against businesses as usual projections. So, in many cases, these commitments are consistent with increasing emissions over the next decade. Many developing countries have set longer-term net zero targets, but in some important cases, such as China, India, and Indonesia, they are beyond the deadline of around 2050 by which the IEA says that net zero is needed. Some of the targets are specifically conditional on international finance.

Here is the view of Poland's Prime Minister, "Europe's emissions of CO_2 is approximately 8% of the entire globe. And if we reduce it by 1% with huge effort, and there is carbon leakage and lots of jobs lost from Europe. And at the same time, in India, China, and Russia, coal power plants are being opened ... it's not making huge sense".[140] This view can certainly be criticised. The example of Europe and other developed economies is hugely important, and it is inevitable that the developing world will lag behind to some degree. But the fact that such opinions are held underlines the point that without progress in the developing world, it becomes harder to maintain consensus for low-carbon transition in the West.

For the developing nations themselves, economic development and raising living standards are the top priorities. They understand the seriousness of the climate challenge and they are willing to follow a low-carbon development path, but not at the expense of economic development and poverty relief. Support from the West has to promote economic growth hand in hand with low-carbon investment. "Climate justice means giving the developing countries enough space to grow", says India's Prime Minister Narendra Modi.[141] Developing countries rightly expect that climate aid should be genuinely additional to existing development aid. Nevertheless, the objectives and challenges of climate aid are closely related to those of development aid.

Climate Justice

The climate negotiations have engendered a vigorous debate on the nature of "climate justice". The main principles advanced as representing Climate Justice have been that, bearing in mind their history of high levels of emissions per person, the developed nations must accelerate their carbon reduction to leave space for the development of poorer nations within the global carbon budget; that developing nations must be allowed sufficient carbon budgets to ensure that climate policies do not impede their economic growth and poverty relief; and that the developed nations must support the transition of developing countries with financial assistance, including compensation for loss and damage, and with the transfer of key technologies.

There is an argument that a nation's total emissions entitlement should be proportional to population. In other words, that everyone on Earth should have their own standard climate budget. There is basic equity in that. It would imply a sharp readjustment of the balance of emissions.

So far we have used up about two-thirds of the carbon budget that is available within a 2°C global warming target, and more than half of those emissions have been from the wealthy developed nations that make up less than 20% of the world's population. Starting from there, it would take a rather drastic readjustment to equalise emissions per head. According to one study, it would cost high-income nations about 6% of GDP per annum in the period leading up to 2050.[142] A significant part of this would be spent on purchasing credits from developing nations. Six percent of the GDP of the OECD is about $3 trillion, which certainly puts into the shade the $100 billion p.a. of promised support that the developed nations have so far failed to deliver.

A somewhat less demanding alternative is the principle that current emissions per head should equalise, also by 2030. The same study estimated that this would cost high-income economies around 3% of GDP. As the US and Europe have now committed to net zero by 2050, while China and India are targeting 2060 and 2070 respectively, it seems likely that this criterion will be satisfied at some time in the first half of this century, but probably not by 2030.

Developing countries, especially India, have argued vigorously for an emissions per head approach at various stages of the negotiations. An early Indian climate commitment was that emissions per head would never exceed the average of the developed nations.[143] That might not seem difficult to achieve, bearing in mind that today India's emissions per head are about an eighth of America's or a fifth of Germany's. However, if the US and Germany are indeed going to achieve net zero by 2050, and India is aiming for 2070, the rule will eventually be broken.

There is an argument that the most efficient way of de-carbonising the world would be for every country to adopt the same price of carbon, enforced through a mixture of taxation, regulation, and subsidies. The most cost-effective carbon reduction measures would be adopted everywhere. However, that might seem to conflict with the principle of "common but differentiated responsibilities" unless the developed countries bore a significant part of the developing nations' costs.

In their analysis of how countries might meet their announced net zero pledges, the IEA assumes somewhat differentiated shadow prices of carbon. In advanced economies, the price rises from \$120 per tonne of CO_2 in 2030 to \$200 in 2050. In developing economies, it rises from \$40 to \$160. Most probably, the developing economies will, indeed, need more time to impose policies that effectively raise the carbon price.

As the Indian Environment Minister said in 2015, "Today I see the carbon space occupied by the developed world. We are asking the developed world to vacate the carbon space to accommodate us. This carbon space demand is climate justice. It is our right as a nation. It is our right as people of India, and we want that carbon space".[144]

In the run-up to the Paris Climate Summit, Prime Minister Narendra Modi said, "Climate justice demands that, with the little carbon space we still have, developing countries should have enough room to grow". But following the summit, he tweeted "Deliberations and Paris agreement demonstrate collective wisdom of world leaders to mitigate climate change" and "Climate justice being won and we are all working towards a greener future".[145]

In his speech to the Glasgow Summit, in which he set out India's new climate targets, Prime Minister Modi criticised the failure of developed countries to provide promised finance and he said, "India expects developed countries to provide climate finance of \$1 trillion at the earliest". He said that India could then agree to bring forward its 2070 net zero commitment. This demand was rejected by UK Prime Minister Johnson.

India's Paris NDC of 2015[146] concludes that, "A preliminary estimate suggests that at least \$2.5 trillion of international climate finance will be required to meet India's climate change actions between now and 2030". The NDC also calls for free access to relevant technologies and cooperation on R&D.

There is a strong obligation on the developed world to speed up its own low-carbon transition so as to leave carbon space for the developing world to transition and also to help developing countries with this transition. That is partly a matter of justice, but it is also a pragmatic necessity since the developing countries have the future of the climate in their hands.

This includes an obligation to increase the provision of green development grants and concessionary finance. But it takes two to tango. Developing countries have to create the conditions where low-carbon investment can flourish. Otherwise, no amount of development aid can achieve the desired result. We have to be creative and develop new forms of green development partnership to enable this to work.

The support that developed nations contribute to the developing world will be vital. That is why it is Key Policy No. 5. However, the example of how richer countries achieve climate transition will also have great influence. Climate virtue begins at home. If the West succeeds in shifting its economies away from fossil fuels, and can demonstrate the advantages of doing so, then it is reasonable to expect that developing countries, suitably supported, will be willing to follow.

The chapters so far have tended to refer to developing countries as a whole. Their circumstances, including their climate challenges, are very diverse. The following sections give very brief summaries of the situations in Africa and in the small island states.

The Example of Africa

Africa contributes only about 3% of world CO_2 emissions today. But its share of world population is 17%, projected by the UN to increase to 40% by 2050. Eighty five percent of Sub-Saharan Africans live on less than $5.50 per day and 35% on less than $2.15, defined by the World Bank as extreme poverty. Nearly a billion Africans lack access to clean cooking, with severe health consequences. Agriculture in Sub-Saharan Africa is particularly at risk from climate change. As Dr Birol, the Executive Director of the IEA, has said, "I find it profoundly unjust that Africa, the continent that has contributed the least to global warming, is the one bearing the brunt of the most severe impacts".[147]

According to the IEA, 12 African countries, including South Africa, representing over 40% of the continent's CO_2 emissions, have committed to net zero by around 2050. Yet today, Africa is experiencing an oil and gas renaissance. Projects worth tens of billions of dollars are proposed in Angola, Ghana, Mozambique, Nigeria, Tanzania, and Uganda, many of them for export to Europe. According to Faten Agaad, senior adviser on Climate Diplomacy and Geopolitics for the African Climate Foundation, "African countries are not receiving financing required for the green transition. That's why we see countries turning to fossil fuels as a way to generate incomes. I mean as we speak, the financing of fossil fuels is three times higher than for green energy, that's $30 billion for fossil fuels compared to $9 billion for green energy.[148]

One example is the East African Crude Oil Pipeline to carry oil from Lake Albert in Uganda to the ocean terminus in Tanzania, being developed by Total and Chinese oil giant CNOOC. It is expected to increase Uganda's total tax revenues by 30–70%. The European Parliament has passed a resolution against it, urging the international community "to exert maximum pressure on Ugandan and Tanzanian authorities, as well as the project promoters and stakeholders", to stop oil activities around Lake Albert. The deputy speaker of the Ugandan national assembly responded that "the resolution is based on misinformation and deliberate misrepresentation of key facts on environment and human rights protection. It represents the highest level of neo-colonialism and imperialism against the sovereignty of Uganda and Tanzania".[149]

It is unreasonable for the West to stand in the way of some of the poorest countries in Africa developing their oil and gas resources. It is also likely to be ineffectual as climate diplomacy. Africa's emissions per head are minuscule compared to those of Europe or the US. The West continues to develop its own oil and gas resources and, especially as it tries to manage without Russian supplies, to look for new sources of supply from around the world. The demand for African oil and gas would hardly exist if the West was not still addicted to these carbon-emitting fuels.

The overwhelming priorities for Africa, and especially Sub-Saharan Africa, are the alleviation of poverty through economic growth and, in the field of energy, extending access to electricity and clean cooking.

There are plenty of opportunities to achieve this through low-carbon investment. Africa has lots of sun and minerals that are needed for low-carbon technology, including more than 40% of the world's reserves of cobalt, manganese, and platinum.

Unfortunately, low-carbon investment in Africa today is on nothing like the scale required. Part of the problem is the indebtedness of many African states. But corruption is also a problem. As the UN Economic Commission for Africa has said, "Corruption is indeed one of the major impediments to structural transformation in Africa". "Corruption cannot be tackled without considering the broader governance challenges in each African country".[150] The problems include "inadequate institutional structures and processes". The solutions include "transparency, participation, accountability, and integrity". The report also points out that Western businesses engaging in corrupt practices for commercial advantage are also a significant part of the problem.

Some of these problems can only be solved from within. But working with African governments, wherever the opportunity arises, to strengthen local institutions and drive out corruption, should be a top priority of Western governments and aid agencies not only in the interests of economic development and poverty relief but also for climate mitigation.

The Example of Small Island States

The Alliance of Small Island States (AOSIS) includes 39 small island and coastal developing countries, some of whose very existence is threatened by climate change. For these countries climate change is indeed an existential threat. They represent the tragic irony that it is countries that have played almost no part in the causes of global warming that are now most at risk. Many of them are located in regions that are subject to tropical storms and have dense populations in low-lying regions that are vulnerable to rising sea levels. For instance, 80% of the land area of the Maldives is within one metre of sea level. As the AOSIS statement to the Glasgow Climate Summit pointed out, "The difference between small island states and industrialized nations is the capacity to respond. It takes a single storm a few hours to destroy the economy and infrastructure of an entire small island state, which lacks the necessary financial and other resources to rebound and rebuild".

The small island states have made their voices heard, and have had a significant impact on climate negotiations. They are calling for a firm commitment to contain global warming within 1.5°, for much increased financial assistance for adaptation as well as mitigation from the developed nations, and for a mechanism to compensate developing nations for loss and damage due to climate change.

Their influence can be seen in the agreement reached at Glasgow which, however, fell well short of meeting their demands. The parties agreed to "pursue efforts" to limit global warming to 1.5°C above pre-industrial levels. They "deeply regretted" the failure of developed nations to deliver the promised $100 billion p.a. of aid by 2020 and they urged the developed countries to significantly increase this support in the future, but without any specific target. They urged developed countries to "at least double" climate finance for adaptation from 2019 to 2025. They set up a "Glasgow dialogue" on funding to "avert, minimise, and address" loss and damage. Small island states were also influential in securing agreement, at Sharm El-Sheikh, to set up a loss and damage fund. Assuming that this fund gets off the ground in a meaningful form they can expect to be major beneficiaries.

The Climate Treaty and Subsequent Agreements

As the title suggests, the 1994 Climate Treaty, strictly the United Nations Framework Convention on Climate Change (UNFCCC), provides a framework for more specific actions. Originally, it was hoped that agreement could be reached on a safe level of future emissions and on a fair distribution of the remaining capacity between nations, a "top down" approach. That approach broke down and, as described in Chapter 1, the 2015 Paris Agreement which is now the basis of climate diplomacy follows a "bottom up" approach. It is up to each country to volunteer its own measures and targets and then, progressively, to "ratchet up". The system has yielded significant gains, but not nearly enough so far.

The Climate Treaty itself contains some significant general principles. The introduction notes that, "the largest share of historical and current emissions has originated in developed countries" and that "per capita emissions in developing countries are still relatively low". The treaty calls for the widest possible cooperation of all countries to meet "common but differentiate responsibilities". This much quoted phrase from the treaty means, among other things, that "the developed country Parties should take the lead". They must provide "new and additional resources" to contribute to the incremental costs of the developing countries. They must also transfer technology.

The treaty recognises that, for developing countries, poverty eradication is the first priority. "The extent to which developing country Parties will effectively implement their commitments under the Convention will depend on the effective implementation by developed country Parties of their commitments under the Convention related to financial resources and transfer of technology and will take fully into account that economic and social development and poverty eradication are the first and overriding priorities of the developing country Parties". A key principle in the treaty is that developed countries must set targets in the form of absolute emission quantities, whereas developing nations have the freedom to set them more flexibly. Developing countries have generally set their medium-term targets either in terms of carbon intensity, in other words, emissions per unit of GDP, or as savings against projected business as usual growth.

These differences were close to the surface at the 2021 Glasgow Climate Summit. The West was unhappy that developing nations would not agree to "phase out" their coal industries, while the developing nations were disappointed by the level of support provided by the West.

The 2022 Climate Summit was chaired and hosted by Egypt, the first developing country to do so. The difference showed. The main topic was the proposal for a new fund through which the developed nations will compensate developing nations for "loss and damage" caused by climate change. After a tough period of negotiation, the developed nations, starting with the EU and eventually including the US, agreed in principle to the creation of such a fund. However, questions, such as how it is to be managed, who will contribute, and how much, all remained to be settled on another day.

Supporting Low-Carbon Transition in the Developing World

Government Aid

The developed and the developing world need to find ways to work together to stimulate rapid low-carbon economic development. Without that, the climate cause is lost. Supporting the developing world is Key Policy No. 5. This is a challenge for business and private financial organisations as much as for governments and government-backed financial and development bodies. In principle, the opportunities for mutual benefit are immense, but in practice, as those who have been working in the field of international development aid have experienced, there are barriers and difficulties to overcome. Ultimately, national low-carbon transformation, like economic transformation, will only be achieved through private sector investment. Therefore, the main purpose of government aid should be to open the door for that to become possible.

There is not only competition between the West and China for leadership in low-carbon transition, but there is also competition for the "hearts and minds" of major developing nations that is pursued, in part, through rival aid offers. The US has been greatly alarmed by the development of China's Belt and Road initiative into a truly massive programme of infrastructure finance for developing nations across Asia, Africa, and South America. Rightly or wrongly, the fear is that America will fall behind in its global influence. Now, the US is promoting its own initiatives for international infrastructure finance, notably the G7 Build Back Better World and, with Japan and Australia, the Blue Dot Network. The EU has its Global Gateway Partnership. Thus, the architecture of development aid is following the fault lines of geopolitical competition. Whether these hopeful new initiatives will ever match the scale of Belt and Road remains to be seen.

According to the IEA, annual capital spending in emerging and developing economies needs to expand to nearly $1 trillion p.a. on clean energy supply plus $450 billion p.a. on low-carbon end use during 2026 — 2030 to put the world on track for net-zero emissions by 2050.[151]

However, not even the $100 billion p.a. target for government-mobilised funds was expected to have been met by 2020, the promised date. According to OECD analysis,[152] total "new and additional" funds mobilised in 2019, the most recent year for which data were available, amounted to $79.6 billion and this was judged unlikely to rise to $100 billion by 2020. Within this total, approximately $20 billion was for adaptation, so the sum available for mitigation was about $60 billion.

There have been other criticisms of this funding besides the overall shortfall. Only $16.7 billion was in the form of government grants. The rest was in the form of loans or export credits. Also, only $3.8 billion was provided through multilateral climate funds, such as the Green Climate Fund and the Global Environmental Facility, set up to support the work of the UNFCCC, and over which developing nations share control with the donors. The donor nations preferred to contribute bilaterally, directly to the beneficiaries ($28.8 billion), or through multilateral development banks, such as the World Bank, where they have a greater degree of control ($30 billion). $14 billion was private sector finance "mobilised" by the public contributions.

One can see the tensions that arise in aid policy through recent developments in the UK. Following a significant cut in the UK's total aid budget, the government merged its aid ministry with its foreign service, creating the Foreign, Commonwealth and Development Office (FCDO). In May 2022, the government announced a decision to spend more through bilateral aid programmes and less through multilateral organisations, such as the World Bank. The Foreign Secretary said, "In an increasingly geopolitical world we must use development aid as a key part of our foreign policy … bringing more countries into the orbit of free market economics".[153] This was supposedly in contrast to "Malign actors" who "treat economics and development as a means of control". Such sentiments help to explain why only a small part of global climate development aid has so far been channelled through the funds established under the Climate Treaty.

To put this into perspective, total development aid, not just climate related, from OECD countries was $161 billion in 2020, of which

$26 billion was loans and equity investments. Over the past five years, the OECD recorded $33 billion of development finance per year from the members of its development committee for energy-related activities. However, disturbingly, 2019 saw Official Development Assistance (ODA) for new fossil fuel infrastructure surpass ODA for renewable energy for the first time since 2015.[154]

The Development Banks

The international finance of development unfortunately reflects the divided world that we live in. The biggest single player in the West is the World Bank Group. In 2021, the group provided nearly $100 billion of new finance, almost all to the developing world, in the form of loans, grants, equity investments, and guarantees. In recent years, about 35% of the World Bank's finance has been in support of climate action, at least 50% of that supporting adaptation.[155]

The World Bank Group claims also to have mobilised $23 billion of private finance in support of its operations and transactions.[156] However, as a useful World Bank blog points out, this may greatly under-estimate the bank's total impact on private investment. This is because it does not take account of private investment that is not part of a specific World Bank project but which results from the bank's work improving the underlying conditions for private sector activity and investment.[157]

In spite of its expansive name, the World Bank remains very much a Western institution. It was formed after World War II as part of the Bretton Woods agreements. Eighteen nations are members, however voting power is related to the finance subscribed. The US alone has 16% of the votes, compared to China with 6% and India with 3%. G7 countries together have 40%. By convention, the President of the World Bank is always an American.

Other International Development Banks (IDBs) have largely followed the World Bank model. The European Bank for Reconstruction and Development (EBRD) was set up after the fall of the Berlin Wall to promote investment in Eastern Europe but has since adopted a broader international remit. As you would expect, its shareholding is dominated by the larger

European countries as well as the US and Japan, though its membership is much wider. In 2021, it invested €10.4 billion, of which €5.4 billion was in the "Green Economy Transition".

The Asian Development Bank (ADB) focuses on the Asia Pacific region. Japan and the US are the largest shareholders and the President is Japanese. In 2020, the ADB committed $22.8 billion in loans, grants, investments, and guarantees, and it has a cumulative climate financing ambition of $100 billion by 2030.

The African Development Bank (AfDB) listed about $6 billion of development aid approvals in 2020. It invests in Africa and voting power is with the large African nations. The largest source of development finance for Latin America is the Inter-American Development Bank (IADB). A majority of the voting rights are with the "borrowing" members from South and Central America, but the US is the largest single shareholder and the HQ is in New York. In 2021, it provided $23 billion in loans, investments, commitments, mobilization, and technical assistance.[158]

At their summit in 2013, the BRICS (Brazil, Russia, India, China, and South Africa) agreed to set up their own investment bank, now called the New Development Bank (NDB). Each BRICS country has equal voting rights. The HQ is in Shanghai and the current president is an Indian. In 2020, it approved $10 billion of loans.

China is not categorised as a developed economy and so has no obligation to provide climate aid under the Climate Treaty,[159] but it has become a major player.

When China launched the Asian Infrastructure Investment Bank (AIIB) in 2014, it was widely viewed with suspicion in the West. China believed, with some reason, that existing institutions had failed to adapt adequately to China's rise as a leading world economy. As described above, the World Bank remains largely a Western institution. The US feared that, besides shifting economic power and influence to China, the AIIB would not abide by international banking norms and undercut the World Bank in terms of economic, social, environmental, and credit standards.

In 2015, the UK became the first Western Nation to become a member of the AIIB, claiming that through early engagement in the Articles of

Association, it had "ensured that the AIIB embodies the best standards in accountability, transparency, and governance".[160] The US was furious. However, since then, the other major European nations have followed the UK's lead.

China is certainly dominant in the AIIB, to an even greater degree than the US is in the World Bank. China has, by far, the largest voting rights of any single country, conferring an effective veto on major decisions. The HQ is in Beijing and the president is Chinese. Nevertheless, the shares are widely held, there is significant Western influence, and the bank is developing transparent and credible environmental and other standards. In 2020 the AIIB approved projects worth $9.8 billion and announced a policy that 55% of its investments will be in "sustainable infrastructure". The US is still not a participant, reflecting heightening international tensions between the US and China.

Belt and Road

By far the most significant Chinese initiative in the field of economic development is Belt and Road. It has been described as "perhaps the most ambitious investment and infrastructure project ever conceived".[161] Belt and Road is at the heart of Xi Jinping's foreign policy, designed to enhance China's international influence as a major world power, to increase its international trade, to bring greater prosperity to China's still relatively impoverished Western provinces, and to provide business for some of China's largest state owned enterprises.

Originally focused on central Asia, Belt and Road has now expanded to cover the whole of the developing world. Belt and Road is not just about energy, but energy projects play a big part. At its heart is a vast infrastructure investment programme covering energy, roads, railways, ports, and, most recently, digital networks. So far, there are $575 billion of projects executed or planned and on some estimates, $1.2–1.3 trillion may have been invested by 2027. The projects are financed by loans from Chinese banks, including development banks, and the projects are, in the main, carried out by China's state-owned enterprises.

Belt and Road may have the scale and impact to significantly enhance the rate of economic development in many parts of the world. But it has been much criticised in the West. In part, this is simply because it may enhance China's international influence, even to the extent of creating economic dependence, at the West's expense. But there are also fears that developing nations may be making financial commitments that are beyond their means.

China prides itself that, in contrast to Western development agencies, it does not attempt to interfere with the domestic policies of sovereign states. One consequence of this has been legitimate concerns about the environmental and social standards of the projects that it supports. A particular worry has been that Belt and Road has until recently been one of the few remaining sources of international finance for coal-fired power stations. However, its stated intention is now to "put green developments in a more prominent position".[162] Speaking to the UN General Assembly in the run-up to the 2021 Glasgow Climate Summit, Xi Jinping said, "We need to forge greater synergy among multilateral development cooperation processes ... China will step up support for other developing countries in developing green and low-carbon energy and will not build new coal-fired power projects abroad".[163]

The show pieces of Belt and Road have been the two meetings of the Belt and Road Forum, held in 2017 and 2019 in Beijing. China pressed for, and achieved, a high level of turn out by the heads of government of participating states and Xi Jinping delivered keynote addresses. However, in 2021, a somewhat lower-key virtual, "Asia and Pacific High-Level Conference on Belt and Road Cooperation" was held, to which Xi Jinping sent only a written address. It is not clear whether this reflects some downgrading of Belt and Road or whether this was simply due to the limitations posed by the COVID-19 pandemic. Recently, in November 2022, Xi Jinping has said that he is considering holding another Belt and Road Forum.

Belt and Road is based on a series of bilateral agreements between China and participating nations, of whom there are now about 70. Belt and Road has no constitution. The forum is simply a high-level meeting, called at China's discretion. Decision-making is entirely in the hands of China. One might say that this is no different from the development aid departments of Western countries, except that Belt and Road claims to be an international partnership. Belt and Road aims to encompass wide-ranging technical, educational and cultural cooperation as well as infrastructure investment, and there is a raft of international Belt and Road organisations on these topics.

According to a recent analysis at Boston University,[164] loans by China's two biggest contributors, the China Development Bank and the Export–Import Bank of China, declined sharply from $75 billion in 2019 to $4 billion in 2020. These two banks provided close to half a trillion dollars in government loans from 2008 to 2021, equivalent to World Bank lending over the same period, so this is certainly a big deal. Others have questioned whether this is the full story.

Whether this signifies that Belt and Road is running down is open to question. Certainly the Belt and Road financing model has run into serious difficulties in countries such as Venezuela, Pakistan, and Sri Lanka, and there have been cancellations and renegotiations in Malaysia, Myanmar, and Russia.[165]

The Belt and Road model is evolving in the light of these problems. China's second Belt and Road Forum in 2019 directed China's financiers to focus on lending to fewer more sustainable projects. Following China's commitment not to fund new coal-fired power stations, the Chinese government have issued guidance on "Making Green a Defining Feature of Belt and Road".[166]

Carbon Trading

International carbon trading represents another possible source of finance for energy transition projects in the developing world.[167] The Glasgow Climate Summit clarified the rules. Countries or businesses falling short on their carbon targets can buy credits from countries with carbon savings to spare. Businesses may also be able to buy credits, an important provision since many businesses are also setting themselves net zero targets.

There are reasons for some caution. A similar scheme under the Kyoto Protocol, known as the Clean Development Mechanism, had a mixed reputation. There was serious doubt whether all the credits generated under the scheme reflected genuinely additional emissions reductions.

Some, but not all, of the left over Kyoto credits will be eligible for trading under the new scheme. The new provisions include a complicated mechanism, including an international oversight body, intended to ensure that credits are "real, additional, and verifiable". These schemes are notoriously difficult to police and these arrangements will take several years to put in place.

The fundamental problem is that under the Paris Agreement, governments set their own emissions targets. Developing nations could, at least in theory, relax their climate targets, compared to what they would otherwise have been, in order to give themselves more credits to sell. In that case, when the purchasing developed nations claimed the credits against their climate targets, the whole process would have led to a net addition in allowable emissions, not at all the original intention.

However, carbon trading does seem likely to generate a significant flow of climate mitigation funding to developing nations. The International Emissions Trading Association (IETA) says that additional finance from carbon markets could exceed $1 trillion by 2050. As developed countries approach net zero, their marginal costs of carbon saving will be a great deal higher than those in developing countries on a slower trajectory. Trading in carbon credits could have big economic benefits. According to a study by the Environmental Defense Fund,[168] carbon trading could reduce the cost of meeting Paris climate pledges by $300–500 billion over 2020–2035. If these costs were re-invested in emissions reduction, they estimate that cumulative emissions reductions over the period would nearly double.

Developing a sound system of international carbon trading is fraught with difficulty. Most importantly, it depends on identifying and supporting good quality low-carbon projects and policies in the developing world. Yet carbon trading is one possible route for channelling substantial clean investment funds to the developing world. Every effort should be made to make it a success.

Making Low-Carbon Development Aid Effective

A substantial increase in climate support from the developed world to the developing world is needed. This should facilitate a much larger increase in private-sector investment. The IEA says that public and private investments in emerging and developing countries needs to increase to nearly $1.5 trillion p.a. It's a big increase. However, this is not simply a matter of opening a financial flood gate. Delivering effective development aid is complex and difficult, as experience has shown, especially for those countries most in need. Climate-related aid is no exception. A large part of development aid in the future will have a climate dimension.

Serious questions have been raised about the effectiveness of today's development aid. There are many problems. The aid itself is poorly coordinated. The developed countries between them have hundreds of aid agencies each with its own strategy and procedures, creating a confusing picture for the host nations. Sometimes aid is tied to supplies or services from the donor country. Aid is not always well coordinated with host country development strategies and is sometimes granted only for short periods with no assurance of continuity. Some have argued that it may help to prop up corrupt regimes and actually displace private-sector investment.

In its 1995 publication on Strengthening the Effectiveness of Aid, the World Bank concluded that, "for aid to be effective, five conditions are essential: ownership by the government and participation by the affected people; strong administrative and institutional capacity; sound policies and good public sector management; close coordination by donors; and improvements in aid agencies' own business practices". It's quite a demanding prospectus. Similar conclusions are in the Paris Declaration on Aid Effectiveness, agreed by most developing and developed countries in March 2005.

Host countries need to have the willingness and capability to benefit from the aid, and aid providers have to work with their governments and other institutions to achieve this. The risks are high and have to be managed by lenders and donors, because taxpayers in donor countries will not tolerate a perception that development aid has been wasted. Some of the highest impact projects also have the highest risk.

Host government policies will have the biggest role in achieving low-carbon growth in the developing world, as they do in the developed world. In most cases, also in common with the developed world, governments have set admirable long term targets, but shorter and medium-term policies to get on the right path are lacking. Developing country governments have said that adequate support from the developed world is a condition for them to follow these policies. They are following the principles of the Climate Treaty. However, in order to deliver this support, aid agencies need host governments to develop their own low-carbon policies and strategies. It has to be remembered that economic development, poverty eradication, and clean energy transition are the ultimate objectives and not the amount of development aid, although increased development aid is an essential element. Proposals for a new international body that would help in the development of such strategies and coordinate the provision of finance are discussed in Chapter 6.

The problem of establishing sound counterparties for public or private sector loans was discussed in Chapter 3. Lenders will be understandably reluctant to put money into the electricity sector in South Africa, for instance, until its power company, Eskom, has been reformed. The weak finances of power distribution companies in India is also a barrier, although the Indian government has been somewhat more successful in supporting alternative investment channels. For many developing countries, energy sector reform will be the key to opening up sources of private finance.

The ambition of the new generation of aid will be to support host governments in achieving a radical change of direction towards low-carbon options. Government policy is central to achieving such a shift. That requires a sophisticated dialogue in which donors and host governments must engage as equals. Western donors have been guilty of rigidly imposing the Washington consensus on host governments. On the other hand Chinese donors, under the principle of non-interference with sovereign states, have tended not to question the suitability of requested prestige projects. Neither approach is appropriate.

The contribution of private finance is vital. Private finance can contribute to project discipline and often comes with the transfer of valuable skills and technology. The supply of private finance is, to all intents and purposes, limitless, for projects with bankable risks and profit margins. Aid institutions, including government agencies and international development banks, are becoming increasingly adept at "mobilising" private capital. An aid agency may negotiate with governments and relevant local participants to set up a development project that then becomes attractive to private lenders. Agencies can bundle projects and spread the risks so that they can be financed by privately funded bonds. There are various other options for mitigating the risks faced by private investors. These include guarantees and structured financings in which the aid agency contributes a tranche of high risk capital.

So it is wrong to be cynical about the desire of lenders to engage private capital. Private capital is the most powerful agent of change. But this is not to diminish the role of government aid agencies and it does not alter the fact that governments will need to greatly increase their resources. All of the above "mobilising" options draw on the resources of aid agencies, their finances and their credit capacity.

It follows that the big international development banks, the World Bank, the EBRD, the ADB, the IADB, and the AIIB, along with national development banks, have a big part to play in achieving low-carbon transition in the developing world. This is where much of the expertise in developing the economies of low-income countries lies.

The Burden of Sovereign Debt

According to the World Bank, in 2021, 60% of low-income countries are at high risk of debt distress or already experiencing it. The 74 IDA countries are those eligible for Economic Development Aid because their national income is less than $1,255 per person. "In IDA countries ratios of debt to gross national income remain well above their levels before the pandemic. With the 2022 growth outlook cut in half, interest rates much higher, and many currencies depreciating, the burden of debt is likely to increase further".[169] Their total international government debt was nearly $1 trillion. Much of that was either to the multilateral aid agencies or to the private sector. Of the bilateral government debt, 32% ($64 billion) was to the developed OECD countries, and 49% ($98 billion) was to China. The debt of all low and middle-income countries was $9 trillion.[170] This level of indebtedness, especially of the very poorest nations, is a serious obstacle to economic development, including the financing of low-carbon transition. Nobody is going to lend money to countries that cannot afford their existing debts. This means that international efforts to provide debt relief for the most indebted low income nations is an integral part of the international climate effort.

The developed nations have an informal organisation, known as the Paris Club, for sharing the pain of debt forgiveness and restructuring. A cardinal principle is that the International Development Agencies, such as the World Bank, should not be expected to participate. That protects the high credit ratings which are essential for their effectiveness. Until recently China has declined to accept this principle and therefore to take part in Paris debt discussions. More recently, in 2023, China has softened its position. Hopefully, this will open the door for a new round of concessions.

Increasing the Contribution of the World Bank

The governments of the West are pressing the World Bank to increase lending to developing countries. US Climate Envoy John Kerry has said that if the World Bank and regional development banks could increase their lending by hundreds of billions of dollars, it could leverage trillions in capital from the private sector and other sources.[171]

Here are the comments of the German economic development Minister, "The World Bank needs to restructure to address the global challenges of the future. Its current model, which is mainly based on demand from borrowing countries, is no longer appropriate in this time of global crises. Challenges and investment needs are so great that the model needs to be adjusted. This means, for example, that the World Bank needs to provide incentives for countries to use its loans to address global challenges. It has to make it more attractive for developing countries to use World Bank loans for climate action and biodiversity conservation. One option would be climate lending on better terms. Another would be targeted budget support for governments which want to pursue policy reforms to make their economies climate neutral. My goal is a World Bank which is well prepared to address global crises such as climate change and which is able to share its knowledge worldwide".[172]

At the Sharm El-Sheikh Climate Summit, Barbados proposed the "2022 Bridgetown Agenda for the Reform of Global Financial Architecture". The agenda is intended to address three problems: "the cost of living crisis stemming from the war in Ukraine and the COVID-19 pandemic, a developing country debt crisis following the pandemic and climate-related disasters, and the climate crisis as the glaciers melt and storms and droughts intensify". It has three elements: the IMF to provide emergency liquidity and the G20 to agree on debt service suspension, an expansion of multilateral lending by $1 trillion, and new multilateral mechanisms to "activate private sector savings for climate mitigation and fund reconstruction after climate disasters". The Agenda has been widely accepted as a framework for international action but it is far from having been implemented to date.

Everyone agrees that the World Bank should try to leverage more private finance with its own lending. Perhaps a breakthrough is possible. However, this idea is not new, and the bank has been trying to achieve this for many years, with limited success. Increasing the bank's own lending without an increase in reserves would lead to a deterioration in the bank's investment-grade credit rating, something that bank officials are reluctant to allow since this could increase the bank's borrowing costs. There may be some flexibility here, but fundamentally governments will have to contribute more to the bank's reserves if they want to achieve a major increase in its lending. Western governments are also urging the bank to change its priorities to spend more on climate mitigation and adaptation and relatively less on other forms of poverty alleviation in the poorest of nations. This is surely a questionable proposition.

One way to increase the assets of the bank would be to allow China shareholding and voting power that is more commensurate with the size of its economy, something that the US has consistently resisted. It is perhaps not surprising that, having been denied such participation, China has largely gone its own way on development finance. A first step in working towards a more integrated approach with China should be to allow China to raise its shareholding substantially.

A more integrated approach between China and the West could help to ensure that finance and support are well directed and, by sharing the risks, increase the total of public and private funds available. This may seem an unrealistic suggestion at a time when tensions between China and the West are increasing. Perhaps so. But Xi Jinping's call for "greater synergy among multilateral development cooperation processes" seems like a positive signal. There are other indications that closer cooperation may be possible.

The first of these is China's change of heart on the financing of coal power overseas, combined with steps to make Belt and Road more environmentally responsive. Then there are the problems that China faces as the lending capacity of its major state banks declines. China needs wider sources of finance to maintain the momentum of Belt and Road. One way to do this would be to give Belt and Road an institutional base that would be more acceptable in the West. This would include an institutional structure in which China, while still the dominant player, shared its leadership with other participants, rather as the US shares its leadership of the World Bank. The participants would then agree on binding guidelines on key topics, such as the environment, the sustainability of finance, project design, and competition between contractors.

In setting up the Asian Infrastructure Investment Bank, China has taken a step towards greater cooperation with the West. The AIIB already has attracted participation from Western European countries, if not, so far, the US or Japan. The report, in July 2023, that the AIIB is to guarantee $1 billion of World Bank sovereign loans is excellent news.

It is already common for international development banks to spread their risks by co-financing major development projects. So far the Belt and Road projects have been financed almost exclusively by Chinese banks. A more international architecture for Belt and Road might enable their projects to also be syndicated with other development institutions, thus increasing the pool of finance available and benefiting from international experience. Belt and Road has a mixed record on the viability of its loans and could perhaps benefit from sharing risk assessments with Western institutions, including the World Bank.

As already mentioned, China also seems to be softening its stance on the Paris Group and the forgiveness or restructuring of the debts of developing nations in debt crisis.

Conclusion

It is not just through development aid that the developed countries influence the development pathways of developing countries. There are other major channels. These include trade policy and especially, now, the proposals of the US and the EU to introduce border carbon adjustments. They also include international carbon trading, which has the potential to channel large sums to low-carbon projects in the developing world.

The failure of the developed world to deliver even the $100 billion per annum of support by 2020 that was promised at the Copenhagen Summit is disappointing. It sits ill with the high-sounding pronouncements on climate change that so many leaders have made. Plainly, more investment is needed.

We need to find more creative ways to manage the risks of investing in developing nations in order to open the door to the massive increase in private investment that is required. A more extensive use of full or partial guarantees by International Development Agencies may be a part of the answer. At the request of African heads of state, the African Development Bank set up an infrastructure investment platform known as Africa50. The aim of Africa50 is to attract private as well as public sector finance for an extensive portfolio of energy and other projects across Africa. It combines project development, project finance, and "support at every stage of the cycle". By linking internationally recognised project management capability with African leadership, such a body may be able to square the circle of creating African projects that meet the priorities of the recipient country while at the same time being attractive to international investors at competitive interest rates. It's an area that needs a lot of work.

For developing countries economic growth and raising living standards are generally the top priorities. Many of them are among the most vulnerable to climate change and they have a legitimate claim on the developed nations. For both practical and ethical reasons, the rich countries should now support the efforts of the less developed world to achieve rapid low-carbon economic growth. That is Key Policy No. 5. The rich nations and the international financial institutions which they control must rapidly and substantially increase their financial, technical, and administrative support. They also need to find creative ways of facilitating the flow of private capital. The Bridgetown Agenda provides the right framework. It combines debt relief for countries in financial crisis, increased multilateral lending, and new mechanisms to activate private savings.

The task is far from being straightforward, as experience has shown. Governments and international financial institutions need to work with host countries to help business and private sector finance to manage the investment risks. Africa50 is an interesting example of an international body working in this area. We need more of this kind of creative thinking. Helping governments to achieve energy sector reforms that will promote sound energy institutions is an important part.

The agreement reached in Glasgow now opens the door for trading in carbon credits that can be beneficial to developed and developing nations. If developed nations are willing to include these credits in their net zero strategies, this could make a highly significant contribution to low-carbon investment in the developing world.

Overall, combined with an increase in climate-related development aid, there is a need for stronger coordination of the efforts of public and private investing institutions of the West and of China with developing countries' own clean development plans. Chapter 6 considers what the institutional base for this might be.

China and the West

Climate change is too big an issue to be separated from geopolitical influences. At the top of these is the relationship between the West, primarily the US, and China. As John Kerry, the US Climate Envoy famously said, "The current climate situation cannot be solved without the full engagement and commitment of China".[173] The importance of this relationship was most obvious in the build up to the 2015 Paris Climate Summit. Presidents Obama and Xi Jinping met in November 2014 and committed themselves to making Paris a success, which was in serious doubt at that time. They agreed that, "the United States of America and the People's Republic of China have a critical role to play in combating global climate change, one of the greatest threats facing humanity. The seriousness of the challenge calls upon the two sides to work constructively together for the common good". They both announced new and significant national targets and urged other nations to follow, which almost all of them did. They also announced a programme of joint research and technical cooperation. This was the springboard for the 2015 Paris Climate Summit.

The merits of the conclusion of the Paris summit are discussed elsewhere, but it was widely seen as successful and the agreement reached has provided the framework for climate diplomacy ever since. The power and influence of the "G2" continues to be vital for driving forward the global climate agenda.

Alas, US support for the Paris Agreement, and for the climate effort in general cannot be taken for granted. President Trump announced that the US would withdraw from the agreement which, he said, "undermines our economy, hamstrings our workers, weakens our sovereignty, and puts us at a permanent disadvantage".[174] The US re-joined as soon as President Biden assumed the presidency in January 2021.

As the rivalry and distrust between China and the US grows, the danger of the US being disadvantaged in relation to China remains a compelling issue of US politics. But the view of the Democrats is almost the opposite of President Trump's. Far from regarding the climate challenge a as burden, they fear that the US will be disadvantaged if it is left behind in the race to adopt advanced low-carbon technology.

In November 2021, the US and China issued their Joint Glasgow Declaration in which they renewed their commitment to work together on climate change and announced the creation of a joint Working Group on Enhancing Climate Action in the 2020s. The working group is to pursue cooperation on policy, technology, and standards.

Unfortunately, this partnership has been threatened by the recent sharp deterioration in relations between the two countries. In the run-up to the 2022 Climate Summit in Sharm El-Sheikh, China's foreign ministry was reported as saying, "Climate change diplomacy between China and the United States cannot be separated from broader political tensions between the two sides, and Washington must take responsibility for the breakdown in talks".[175] The relationship remains fragile.

Most of those "tensions" have nothing to do with climate change and are well beyond the scope of this book, but some are in the climate sphere. Under the original Climate Treaty, and its articulation of "common but differentiated responsibilities", China was classified as a developing nation and did not accept the obligations of developed nations to provide international climate aid. China maintains this status even though it now has the second largest economy in the world, and on some measures the largest. China's GDP per head is still well below that of the relatively rich OECD countries, so its status is debatable. It means that China is not expected to contribute to the $100 billion p.a. of climate aid promised by the developed nations, although China also does not expect to be a beneficiary.

China has allied itself with the G77 group of developing nations in the climate talks and was a leading proponent of the Loss and Damage fund, which was eventually agreed upon at Sharm El-Sheikh. However, as a developing nation, China is not intending to contribute. Everything about this fund is yet to be negotiated, so possibly China will change its mind. China's non-contribution to these funds will make it more difficult for the US, and the West more widely, to be generous.

There is also a divide between China and the West on development aid more generally, discussed above. China is the largest bi-lateral lender to the developing world, so its policies are important. So far, the West has resisted giving China a role at the World Bank Group commensurate with the size of its economy, and China has largely gone its own way on development finance, especially through the Belt and Road investment programme. Better cooperation between China and the West, including a more international constitution for Belt and Road could increase the resources available to the World Bank and broaden the basis for risk sharing in developing world investments. China has to some extent had its fingers burnt with Belt and Road and we should not rule out the possibility that China is now interested in a more internationalist approach to development aid. It is well worth exploring what Xi Jinping intended when he called for closer "synergies".

Paradoxically, the rivalry between China and the West can also be a positive force.

As the momentum of energy transformation gathers pace, there is a growing sense that it represents the future and that countries that are left behind will lose out economically and in terms of soft power. That is a powerful motivation that applies, especially, to countries and regions such as the US, China, and Europe that aspire to world leadership. Low-carbon technology has become a major factor in the struggle for world economic and political leadership.

US Secretary of State Antony Blinken has said, "It is difficult to imagine the US winning the long-term strategic competition with China if we cannot lead the renewable energy revolution". As discussed in Chapter 3, fear of falling behind China has motivated, at least in part, President Biden's huge new spending programme on clean energy under the Inflation Reduction Act which, itself, now seems to be stimulating a new round of government investment in low-carbon technology in Europe.

The impacts of this "strategic competition" on the global climate effort are not all favourable. Like any economic endeavour, the low-carbon transition benefits from free trade in products, materials, and technology. Some of the cost reductions of low-carbon technologies have been based on imports from China. As the US places restrictions on trade with China, and the "made in America" requirements of the Inflation Reduction Act take effect, there will be a price to pay in terms of the costs of these technologies and the rate of technical progress, a topic that is discussed further in the following. The West has a legitimate need to protect national security and to reduce its dependence on China for key materials and products where China has a quasi-monopoly, but it should avoid restrictions that go further.

The support of both China and the US is vital for the climate effort. Without either one of these countries, its credibility is significantly undermined and the pressure on other countries to participate is reduced. When China and the US act together, they are a highly effective force for global change, whereas if wider geopolitical tensions are carried over into the climate sphere, notwithstanding some benefits from competition, there is bound to be a loss of global momentum.

China's commitment to "carbon neutrality" by 2060, announced by Xi Jinping at the UN in 2020, seems to have been a "top down" initiative by the president himself made to support China's standing in international climate diplomacy, underlining the importance of China's engagement in the process.

There are two areas where the West could act to improve relations with China on climate change.

The first is to allow China to participate and have voting rights at the IMF and the World Bank that are much more commensurate with the scale of China's economy. The second is to allow China to become a full member of the IEA. Fears have been voiced that this would make it more difficult to pursue the objectives of the West in these organisations, but it is reasonable to set these aside in view of the magnitude of the climate crisis. Similar issues arose over the creation of the G20 in which China is a full and equal participant, but they were overcome because China's contribution was seen as essential to solve the 2008 global financial crisis.

China has been actively involved in international cooperation with countries of the West on policies and technologies for energy transition, for instance, at the Clean Energy Ministerial, at Project Innovation, and through China's association with the IEA. The West should promote this engagement and, as already mentioned, enter into negotiations with China towards full IEA membership. The eventual aim should be to engage China in stronger institutions for cooperation on climate transition as outlined in the following chapter.

The news is not all bad. Following a period of frozen diplomatic relations between the US and China, US climate envoy John Kerry visited China in July 2023.[176] He said that in his discussions both sides had agreed to work to "guarantee a positive outcome" to COP 28 the following December, that they had agreed to resume discussions and that future talks would help them both to develop new climate targets to be submitted in 2025. Perhaps their minds were concentrated by the fact that China recorded temperatures as high as 52°C during the visit. If the G2 is indeed back in harness, that is very good news for the next rounds of climate talks. However, there was no joint statement, and during the visit, Xi Jinping pointedly declared that

China's policy "must be determined by the country itself rather than be swayed by others".

The West has a delicate path to pursue with China on climate change. The West cannot afford for cooperation on climate change to become a bargaining chip for China to demand concessions in other areas. And the West also has to protect its vital strategic interests. However, subject to these two points, the West has every reason to pursue closer cooperation with China on climate change leadership, cooperation, and development finance.

Chapter 6

Strengthening World Governance for Implementation

Key Policy No. 6.

The UNFCCC is the one legitimate body for climate negotiations and for the setting of climate targets. But there is a lack of international cooperation for delivering those targets. We need to raise the level of global cooperation on implementation. That is Key Policy No. 6. This could be achieved by strengthening the International Energy Agency (IEA) and widening its membership. The creation of an altogether new body, as outlined in the Appendix, would be more ambitious.

Introduction

More attention needs to be given to the global governance of climate mitigation. The Climate Treaty remains the legitimate forum for top-level negotiation. In many ways, it has been remarkably successful. It is primarily concerned with the exchange of top-level climate targets. There is much less focus on delivering the policies needed to achieve those targets, and there is limited continuity between top-level climate meetings. After each Climate Summit, the "captains and the kings depart", hoping that the targets that they have announced have done enough to protect their green reputations, but they are not engaged in meaningful international dialogue on the steps to achieve them.

An international body is needed that can give sustained and strategic coordination to the low-carbon energy transition, focusing on the delivery of climate targets. This needs to bring together the analysts, the funders, and the host governments with national climate envoys. In some ways, this would be analogous to the UK's Climate Change Committee, but on a global stage. None of the existing organisations meets this need. It might be met through a reform and enhancement of the IEA, or through the creation of a new body. The creation of new international organisations, or the reform of existing ones, is a tough diplomatic undertaking. The bar is high. But in view of the magnitude of the climate threat the effort is required and justified. Reforming the IEA, although challenging, is the more realistic objective, and recent communiques from the IEA's Governing Board suggest that thoughts are turning in that direction. The following narrative focuses on IEA reform.

Governments are setting demanding long term targets, in many cases to achieve net-zero emissions. The Paris Agreement requires that they be updated every five years. But there is a serious question mark as to whether governments have the short- and medium-term policies that will be needed to achieve them. There needs to be continuous international engagement not only on top-level targets but also on delivery.

The process of delivery is bound to remain "bottom up" in the same way as target setting. Sovereign governments will run their own energy policies. But international engagement is needed for several reasons. First of all, since climate mitigation is inherently a cooperative endeavour, it is reasonable that governments should have to convince their peers from other countries that they have credible plans. Since governments face similar policy options and have to make assumptions about the cost and accessibility of many of the same technologies, there is much to be gained from cross-fertilisation. The plans of developing countries are likely to depend on the availability of finance and other kinds of international support. Therefore, a centre is needed in which developing country plans can be discussed with donor governments, international financial institutions, and representatives of private capital, and credible support plans put in place. Climate aid today is notoriously fragmented.

Existing Organisations

There is no shortage of international organisations and events concerned with energy and climate change; they are as countless as the stars. But none is able to perform the strategic function that is needed.

The G20 has been active on climate change, among many other areas. It can be highly effective in situations where top-level decisions are required to deal with a crisis. For instance, it took effective steps to respond to the financial crisis of 2008, coordinating efforts to enhance global liquidity, and establishing the Financial Stability Board. The G20 could initiate a new organisation, but it cannot itself run a sustained international programme such as is proposed here because it has no permanent secretariat and the chairmanship, and therefore to a large extent the agenda, changes every year.

In recent years, the G20 has held meetings of Energy Ministers and has two groups of senior officials of special relevance to energy, the Energy Transitions Working Group, and the Climate Sustainability Working Group.

The UNFCCC is the accepted, and only, legitimate international organisation for climate negotiations. It meets every year sometimes at the head of government level. The Paris Agreement of the UNFCCC is the recognised framework for climate negotiations. The UNFCCC presides over a complex set of agreements covering the reporting of national climate targets, carbon trading, and the "common but differentiated" obligations of developed and developing nations. There is a considerable architecture of bodies supporting the UNFCCC. These include its secretariat, based in Bonn (Germany), charged with the "analysis and review of climate change information" as well as organising the high-level meetings. There is a Green Climate Fund and a Global Environment Facility. These bodies have a significant and growing role in international climate finance, but for the most part, contrary to the urgings of the UNFCCC itself, donor nations have chosen to channel most of their support through bilateral aid or International Development Agencies, such as the World Bank.

Among many other UNFCCC bodies, there is a Technology Mechanism and a Climate Technology Centre and Network, intended to help developing countries meet their technology needs. These bodies have useful, but at present fairly modest, roles.

The UNFCCC in many ways is an extraordinarily successful organisation. It did not succeed in creating a top-down mechanism for negotiating national emissions quotas. But the Paris framework for voluntary target setting must be rated as a remarkable achievement, even if the outcome still falls short of what is needed.

However, the UNFCCC is focused almost entirely on top-level, and increasingly long term, target setting, and on the highly complex organisation of climate summits. Leaders announce their targets and then, effectively, go away until the next target-setting round. There is no equivalent focus on the energy policies, finance, and technologies needed to meet those targets. That is a particular weakness at a time when there is growing concern about the credibility of demanding net zero targets that governments are setting for several decades into the future.

The IEA is the main international body for energy policy analysis. As climate change has risen on the geopolitical agenda it has taken a leading role in projecting future energy-related emissions and advocating the energy policies that are needed to bring them into line with global objectives. The IEA is now the key international forum for cooperation on energy policy. Its annual flagship publication, World Energy Outlook, is the reference work for international energy analysis and projections. Some 6,000 experts from across the world are engaged in the IEA's technology groups. And the IEA has a transition programme for advising developing nations, including China, on their low-carbon policies. All this makes it, after the UNFCCC, by far the most important international institution for enabling nations to work together on emissions reduction.

The main weakness of the IEA as a global energy body is that only the developed OECD countries can be full members. The IEA could provide the sustained and strategic coordination that is required for the delivery of climate targets provided that it opened its doors fully to developing nations and forged a close alliance with international development banks and other sources of finance. Reform of the IEA is discussed in the following.

Other major organisations concerned with energy include the International Renewable Energy Agency, the Clean Energy Ministerial, which is hosted at the IEA and promotes the development and deployment of clean energy technologies, and Project Innovation, which promotes clean energy R&D.

The International Energy Forum, with its secretariat in Riyadh (Saudi Arabia), has the most comprehensive membership. It meets every other year at ministerial level and its primary role has been to promote dialogue between oil producers and consumers.

The Energy Charter was set up after the collapse of the Soviet Union to encourage energy sector investment in the newly independent states. It is based on a binding treaty intended to protect international energy investments from expropriation or equivalent measures. Most of the members are in Eastern and Western Europe and Central Asia. The treaty has become an embarrassment, at least in Western Europe, because protecting fossil fuel investments is no longer the priority. The EU, which was the driving force behind the creation of the Charter Treaty, is now looking for ways to get out.

None of these bodies is able to perform the strategic role that is needed for overseeing the delivery of national clean energy transition plans. The gap is illustrated by the plethora of one-off high-level meetings that preceded the Glasgow Climate Summit. These included the IEA Clean Energy Transition Summit, the Major Economies Forum on Energy and Climate, the UN High-Level Dialogue on Energy, the High Ambition Coalition on Climate Change, the Net Zero Producers Forum, the COP 26 Energy Transition Council, and the Berlin Energy Transition Dialogue. The leaders come, they declare their fervent commitment to reducing emissions, they may even agree on a document, and then they go away and nothing much changes. To be generous, perhaps they contribute to the general momentum for change. To be less generous, "Blah, Blah, Blah".

There are other bodies with agendas that suggest that they are trying to address the need for sustained strategic coordination. The UNDP Energy Hub aims to "close the gap on delivering Sustainable Development Goal (SDG) No. 7 as a pathway to meeting the 2030 SDGs".[177] Goal No. 7 is for "affordable clean energy". Other SDGs include the eradication of poverty and action on climate change. The Hub plans to "forge strategic relations with G7 and G20 countries, International Financial Institutions, the EU Commission, the UN system as a whole, and private sector organisations".

The World Bank's Energy Sector Management Assistance Program (ESMAP) is a "partnership between the World Bank and 24 donor countries and institutions to help low and middle-income countries reduce poverty and boost growth through sustainable energy solutions". So far, the donors have pledged about half a billion dollars. These are useful institutions, but they are not operating on a scale, or with sufficiently high-level leadership, to exercise a strategic role over the climate effort.

Reform of the IEA

The IEA was founded in 1974, as an oil security pact of the West faced with the Arab oil embargo. Its founding document and current legal basis, the agreement on an International Energy Program,[178] is primarily concerned with the maintenance and emergency use of oil stocks. The agreement restricts IEA membership to the developed OECD countries. Virtually all developed nations belong. The US has a leading role and, by convention, always appoints the Deputy Executive Director. The IEA has its own Governing Board made up of senior officials and sometimes Energy Ministers of its member countries, and controls its own agenda. But administratively it is embedded in the OECD.

Over the years, the IEA has evolved, with remarkable flexibility, to address the changing global priorities for energy policy. However, it retains its important oil security role and membership is still restricted to the OECD.

Now that most of the world's energy demand and greenhouse gas emissions are in developing non-OECD countries, the limitation on membership is a big drawback for an organisation that sets out to be the world's energy adviser. In an effort to address this problem, the IEA has created an association to which 13 mainly developing nations, including China, India, Brazil, Indonesia, and South Africa, now belong.[179] It has worked usefully with all these countries on their low-carbon strategies in a Clean Energy Transition Programme. The association has been a big success. But association members have no voting power at the IEA and they do not sit on the Governing Board, nor do they accept the responsibilities of IEA members. Their status, therefore, is significantly below that of full membership.

The IEA could evolve into the kind of organisation that is needed to coordinate national low-carbon energy strategies. But to do so, it would have to admit developing nations to full membership. It would also need to forge a much closer alliance with international financial institutions.

Unfortunately, for many years, the IEA member countries have been unable to agree on opening up to enable developing countries to become full members. At its 2020 Ministerial level meeting the IEA decided to develop a framework of "strategic partnership" for non-OECD countries wishing to go beyond the association "including potential paths to eventual membership". This cautious language plainly covered continuing doubts among some members. "If the trumpet give an uncertain sound, who shall prepare himself for battle?"[180]

At the 2022 meeting of the Governing Board, there still seems to have been limited progress. Ministers concluded, "We agree that there should be a pathway for IEA membership for like-minded countries willing to make the commitments to the mission and objectives of the IEA, including the IEA Shared Goals and the objectives embodied in this communique. We commit to pursue a bilateral arrangement between the IEA and India under Article 63 that would be negotiated in the final stages of the Strategic Partnership. We direct the Governing Board to elaborate further details of the bilateral arrangement".

The Article 63 referred to says that the IEA "may establish appropriate relations with non-participating [i.e. non-member] countries". It is far from clear that this could cover actual membership. The Shared Goals was a set of IEA objectives adopted by the Governing Board in 1993.

However, the 2022 Ministerial communique also includes a passage that could be highly significant for the future of the IEA and, indeed for global energy governance more widely. The unusually long communique includes a wide-ranging review of international energy policy with an emphasis on climate objectives and concludes, "In light of these mandates, and their impact on the mission, priorities, and operations of the IEA, we may opt to analyse the need for a review of the IEA's underlying Agreement on an International Energy Program. We emphasize that opting to do so neither pre-judges the conclusions of such a review or exploration, including the possibility of leaving the Agreement unchanged, nor delays the implementation of the mandates in this communique".

The communique continues, “We further decide that we may opt to explore the potential utility of a special activity organized under Article 65 of the Agreement to support countries in an orderly clean energy transition, building on the strengths of the current Association model and Clean Energy Transition Programme”.

There appear to be three alternatives under consideration: further development of the association short of membership, membership for some non-OECD countries without changing the agreement, or a review of the agreement itself.

IEA members have already overridden the membership provision of the Agreement. At an early stage in the IEA's life it seemed highly desirable to include Norway, as a friendly oil producer. However, Norway was unwilling to sign the Agreement designed for oil importing countries. The members simply ignored the Agreement and gave Norway all the rights of membership without asking them to sign up for it. Norway is referred to as a member in all IEA publications, although the legal basis for this is questionable. This was not supposed to create a precedent, but obviously, the IEA could do the same thing again if the members so wished. The example of Norway shows that the question of membership is ultimately political rather than legal.

Reviewing the IEA's founding agreement would be a major diplomatic initiative. The existing text is almost entirely about oil security. It contains nothing on climate change and next to nothing on the environment. It was written before developing countries such as China and India became major players. In theory, the agreement could be revised just to change the membership rules, but it seems unlikely that the members would agree to that. Most probably, a revised treaty would have to set out today's international energy policy objectives and the IEA's role in achieving them. It would need to disentangle the IEA from the OECD at least sufficiently to enable non-OECD countries to join.

That is a tough undertaking, especially as unanimity is required for all changes to the Agreement. But circumstances make it necessary.

It is extraordinary that the West still excludes China and other developing nations from full membership of the IEA. We know that we need China's cooperation to achieve global climate objectives and China has shown, on key occasions, that it is willing to cooperate. The reasons given for excluding China are all second order. They mostly relate to the history of the IEA when it was founded as an oil security club for Western oil importers. Now, the IEA has moved on and claims a vital global role.

India is probably closer to full IEA membership than China. When Prime Minister Modi visited the US in June 2023, he and President Biden, "reaffirmed their support for the mission of the IEA, and President Biden pledged to continue working with the Government of India, IEA members, the IEA Secretariat, and other relevant stakeholders toward IEA membership for India in accordance with the provisions of the Agreement on an International Energy Program (IEP)".[181] There is a contradiction here, because the IEP explicitly excludes non-OECD countries, such as India, from IEA membership. But the statement is important because it suggests that the US is not now averse to widening IEA membership.

The history of the G20 is instructive. The first G20 summit was held in 2008. Prior to that, the G7 group of developed nations had been the senior international body. But when the financial crisis occurred, it became clear that the G7 group was insufficient and that China's help was needed to avert a collapse. So China joined along with other leading developing nations. Nobody now regrets that decision, which has given China a voice more commensurate with the scale of its economy. The same arguments apply now to China and the IEA. We need China's help to avoid disaster.

China is not knocking on the door to join the IEA. China appears quite happy with its current role as an association member. That provides many of the benefits but none of the responsibilities of membership. It will take a negotiation to bring China in as a full member, but once China has joined, it is reasonable to expect that other leading developing nations will follow suit. That is what happened when China joined the Association. President Biden has now declared his support for India to join. At present, India is more interested than China in full membership. But Indian membership could be a helpful first step towards admitting China.

The position taken by the US, as the leading participant in the IEA, will be crucial. In August 2023, after a period of frosty relations between the US and China, there appears to have been a slight thaw, at least to the extent that high-level diplomatic exchanges have resumed. The US remains clear that cooperation with China is essential for climate mitigation and appears willing to separate this issue out from more contentious topics. Wider geopolitical tensions may make it difficult to open the door for China to be offered membership in an organisation which remains the West's collective defence on oil security. If that is indeed a barrier, it may be necessary to distinguish membership of the oil emergency mechanisms from membership of the IEA as a whole.

Revision of the IEA's treaty offers the possibility that the IEA could play a much more central role in achieving net zero. Under the new treaty, members would commit to their net zero targets and to the IEA's role in helping them to achieve them and also to the IEA monitoring and reporting on progress. For developing countries, the IEA would need to acquire close relations with funding agencies so that they could also play a coordinating role in finance.

The IEA is particularly fitted for this role because it has an enviable reputation among developing as well as developed nations for technically sound and non-political analysis.

In December 2022, the German Chancellor announced the agreement of the G7 to set up a Climate Club "to support the rapid implementation of the Paris Agreement". Presumably, this builds on the proposals, discussed above, previously put forward by German ministries. The idea was that developed and developing countries would reach agreements through the club on the rate of low-carbon transition of the developing country together with the support to be granted and how the domestic policies of the developed country, such as Carbon Border Adjustment Mechanisms, would affect the developing country. A secretariat for the club is to be established by the IEA and the OECD. At the moment, in May 2023, very little is known about how the club will operate. It could be a useful step towards focusing global efforts to coordinate the climate effort at the IEA.

Conclusion

Much closer international cooperation is needed on policies, programmes, and technologies for achieving climate objectives. This includes working with developing countries to deliver their low-carbon strategies for economic growth and poverty reduction. This requires a strategic approach and appropriate organisation is needed. It will take a major diplomatic effort to put the necessary mechanisms in place. In normal times, that would be considered unrealistic. But these are not normal times. These are essential changes to measure up to the magnitude of the climate challenge. Reform of the IEA seems the most realistic way forward. Creating an altogether new body would represent an even greater challenge. The outline of such a body is set out in the Appendix.

Appendix to Chapter 6

A New International Body for the Delivery of Energy Transition

The alternative to reforming the IEA would be to create a new body. It might be called the International Energy Transition Centre (IETC) for want of a better name. Because of its near universal membership, the UN offers a high level of legitimacy, so it would make sense for the centre to be a UN associate body.[182] It will need sustained high-level political leadership. All UN members would be invited to sit on the governing board, represented by ministerial level climate envoys.

There would be a smaller Executive Committee consisting of equal numbers of donor countries, including China, and developing nations receiving support (host nations). Members of the Executive Committee would be elected from time to time by all the donor countries and host nations, respectively. Also represented on the Executive Committee would be the IEA, the major international development banks, such as the World Bank, and representatives of private capital. It would be up to the Chinese government to decide how Belt and Road was represented. There would need to be a substantial Secretariat formed at least in part by secondees from the institutions and governments represented on the Executive Committee. The Executive Committee would appoint a chair and an executive secretary to head the Secretariat.

The centre would function through task forces, pulling together the relevant governments, financing institutions, and the IEA to agree on the financing of national transition plans and policies. The aim would be to follow the transition plans of sovereign host governments with a minimum of interference. However, they would have to conform to general environmental guidelines to be approved by the Executive Committee. They would also have to be financeable, which would be at the heart of the negotiations.

There are some similarities to the Financial Stability Board (FSB), set up by the G20 to address the financial crisis of 2008. Like the proposed centre, its essential role is to coordinate the work of various national and international organisations. The FSB is located at the Bank for International Settlements (BIS) and reports to the G20, whereas the centre would be located at the UN and report to its General Assembly. However, the G20 could take the initiative in setting up the centre and the centre would be expected to have a continuing relationship with the G20.

How realistic is this proposal? The creation of the centre would have to be associated with a substantial increase in climate support provided by the developed nations, otherwise the developing nations would be unlikely to agree. However, such an increase is essential to the achievement of climate goals and, in agreeing to it, the developed nations may well seek some strengthening of institutional arrangements to ensure its effectiveness.

The proposal assumes a willingness on the part of China to accept closer coordination with the West on its climate-related support, including through Belt and Road. A degree of optimism is needed. However, as discussed above, there are already signs that China may be willing to adopt a more international approach.

There is, rightly, a high hurdle for the creation of new international bodies. Governments worry about the significant cost of the Secretariat and the drain on their officials' time of attending more international meetings. Even more, they shrink from the diplomatic effort needed to secure international agreements. That also has its opportunity cost. However these difficulties have to be set against the immensity of the climate challenge.

Postscript: Geoengineering, a Looming Question

Finally, we should be honest with ourselves. We are far from being on course to limit global warming to 1.5° and even the target of 2° seems difficult. That is a reason to redouble our efforts to avoid even greater disaster. But we should also consider the implications of not reaching these targets.

As concern increases that we may not succeed in limiting greenhouse gas concentrations to safe levels, interest has grown in alternative ways of limiting global warming through geoengineering, defined by the UK's Royal Society as "the deliberate large-scale manipulation of the planetary environment". Many possibilities exist but the most commonly referred to include the release of sulphur aerosols into the stratosphere, which would reduce solar radiation on Earth in the same way that volcanic eruptions do, and seeding the oceans with iron to stimulate the growth of CO_2 absorbing plankton.

This is a highly sensitive topic, where much caution is required. "Fools rush in where angels fear to tread".[183] There are strongly held views. For some geoengineering is a hubristic interference with nature that we should not even contemplate. Others fear that it is an escape clause that risks undermining the effort to reduce our own greenhouse gas emissions. It is certainly the case that, in the absence of further research, we do not fully understand, and might not be able to control, the ultimate consequences of the main geoengineering options. For instance, putting sulphur into the atmosphere may have unpredictable local weather impacts and could threaten the ozone layer, while seeding the oceans will have major consequences for marine life. Some argue that even research into the topic should be anathema on the grounds that it confers unwanted legitimacy and may put us on a slippery slope that will inevitably lead to deployment.[184]

The Climate Treaty does not deal with geoengineering. Some more specialised agreements, such as the Convention on Biological Diversity and the London Convention on the Prevention of Marine Pollution, are relevant to particular geoengineering options. But so far there is no overall global framework to control or grant legitimacy to such interventions.

The UK's Parliamentary Select Committee on Science and Technology has adopted some criteria, known as the Oxford Principles, that were proposed by an *ad hoc* expert group. These specify that geoengineering should be regulated as a public good on behalf of mankind, that there should be public participation, that research should be transparent and independently assessed, and that there should be no deployment until a suitable governance structure is in place.[185]

The ideal regulatory structure might be an umbrella UN convention associated with the Climate Treaty which included roles on specific geoengineering options for relevant specialist international bodies, such as the two conventions mentioned above. There is no early prospect that such a structure will be put in place. There is a high bar for the creation of new international treaties and in this case the challenge is made all the more difficult by the fact that many people have a strong aversion even to discussing the topic.

However, the consequences of climate change are becoming all too evident in many parts of the world. The day may not be so very far off when they become insupportable for one or more countries. There is a risk that those countries might consider unilateral action. The main geoengineering options are not so difficult or costly as to be beyond the reach of any major nation with advanced technical capabilities. But such a step would be fraught with danger for the global environment. That is why it is not too soon to start considering the need for a global treaty that would govern geoengineering.

Glossary

ADB	Asian Development Bank
AIIB	Asian Infrastructure Investment Bank
AOSIS	Alliance of Small Island States
BECCS	Bioenergy with carbon capture and storage
CBAM	Carbon Border Adjustment Mechanism
CCC	Climate Change Committee (of the UK)
CCS	Carbon Capture and Storage
CCUS	Carbon Capture Use and Storage
Climate Summit	Conference of the Parties to the UNFCCC
Climate Treaty	United Nations Framework Convention on Climate Change (UNFCCC)
COP	Conference of the Parties to the UNFCCC
CSP	Concentrating Solar Power
EBRD	European Bank for Reconstruction and Development
EPA	Environmental Protection Agency (of the US)
EPR	European Pressurised Reactor
ETS	Emissions Trading System
FoE	Friends of the Earth
FSB	Financial Stability Board (of the G20)
G77	Group of (Originally) 77 Developing Nations
GDP	Gross Domestic Product
Gt	Gigatonne (= 1 Billion Tonnes)
HGV	Heavy Goods Vehicle
IADB	Inter-American Development Bank
IATA	International Air Transport Association
IEA	International Energy Agency
IIJA	Infrastructure Investment and Jobs Act (of the US)
IPCC	Intergovernmental Panel on Climate Change (of the UN)

IRA	Inflation Reduction Act (of the US)
IRENA	International Renewable Energy Agency
ITER	International Thermonuclear Experimental Reactor
LED	Light-Emitting Diode
MIT	Massachusetts Institute of Technology
Mt	Million Tonnes
MWh	Megawatt Hour
NGO	Non-Governmental Organisation
OECD	Organisation for Economic Co-operation and Development
OPEC	Organization of the Petroleum Exporting Countries
PV	Photovoltaics
PWR	Pressurised Water Reactor
SDG	Sustainable Development Goal (of the UN)
SMR	Small Modular Reactor
SUV	Sports Utility Vehicle
TCFD	Task Force on Climate Related Fiscal Disclosure (of the FSB)
TWh	Terawatt Hour (One Billion Kilowatt Hours)
UAE	United Arab Emirates
UNFCCC	United Nations Framework Convention on Climate Change
VHTR	Very High Temperature Reactor

Endnotes

Introduction

1 The United Nations Framework Convention on Climate Change (UNFCCC).

2 *Ibid.*

3 *UNFCCC Secretariat*, March 2023, UNFCCC summary report following the second meeting of the technical dialogue of the first global stocktake under the Paris Agreement.

4 WHO COVID-19 Dashboard, accessed 30 May 2022.

5 IEA, *Global Emissions Rebound to Their Highest Level in History in 2021*, 8 March 2022.

6 International Renewable Energy Agency (IEA), *World Energy Transitions Outlook*, 2022.

Chapter 1

7 IEA, *World Energy Outlook*, 2021.

8 Eliot, T.S., *The Hollow Men.*

9 Neil A.C., Hirst *The Energy Conundrum, Climate Change, Global Prosperity, and the Tough Decisions We Have to Make*, World Scientific Publishing, 2018.

10 IPCC, *Summary for Policy Makers*, 2022.

11 CNN, 1 November 2021, Biden says climate crisis is "The existential threat to human existence as we know it".

12 UN Press Release, 10 September 2018.

13 Molina, M., *et al.*, Bulletin of Atomic Scientists, *Climate Reports Understate Threat*, 9 October 2018.

14 Synthesis Report of the IPCC Sixth Assessment Report, *Summary for Policymakers*, 2023.

15 *The 2022 Report of the Lancet Countdown on Health and Climate Change*, 25 October 2022.

16 IPCC, *Special Report on Global Warming of 1.5°C*, Revised January 2019.

17 *BBC News*, 28 September 2021, Greta Thunberg mocks world leaders at Youth4Climate.

18 The United Nations Framework Convention on Climate Change (UNFCCC), referred to as "The Climate Treaty" throughout.

19 Our World in Data, CO_2 Emissions.

20 US National Oceanic and Atmospheric Administration (NOAA), *Trends in Atmospheric Carbon Dioxide.*

21 US National Aeronautics and Space Administration (NASA), *Vital Signs of the Planet.*

22 IEA, *Greenhouse Gas Emissions From Energy — Data Explorer, 2021.*

23 IEA, *World Energy Balances*, 2021.

24 Yamana, N. and Guilboto, J., *CO_2 Emissions Embodied in International Trade and Domestic Final Demand, Using the OECD Inter-Country Input-Output Database*. OECD, 2020.

25 Boswell, J., *Life of Samuel Johnson*, 1791. Johnson was commenting on a man's re-marriage after the death of his wife in a previous unhappy marriage.

26 Forbes Wheels, *Trucks, SUV, Car Sales: Winners and Losers*, Updated 7 January 2021.

27 IEA, *World Energy Outlook, 2016.* Figure 2.7 and text.

28 The Intergovernmental Panel on Climate Change (IPCC).

29 *IPCC Special Report on Global Warming of 1.5°C*, October 2018.

30 UN Release, *IPCC Report "Code red" for Human Driven Global Heating, Warns UN Chief*, 9 August 2021.

31 *BBC News, EU leaders set 55% target for CO_2 emissions cut*, 21 April 2021.

32 White House Statement, 22 April 2021.

33 *BBC News*, 17 November 2021.

34 Politico, *EU Will not Strengthen Climate Action Plan in 2022*, 1 December 2021.

35 IEA, *World Energy Outlook* 2022.

36 IEA, *Commentary*, 4 November 2021.

37 *Reuters*, 13 July 2023, US "under no circumstances" will pay climate reparations, Kerry says.

38 *Financial Times*, 14 January 2023, New COP 28 President wants renewable energy generation to triple by 2030.

39 IEA, *World Energy Investment*, 2023.

40 *The Guardian*, 24 July 2023, Rishi Sunac says net zero strategy must be "proportional and pragmatic".

Chapter 2

41 IEA, *Energy Efficiency*, 2022.

42 *Ibid.*

43 IEA, Renewables 2021, analysis and forecasts to 2026 climate change 2021, The physical science basis, summary for policymakers.

44 IEA, *World Energy Outlook*, 2021.

45 MIT Energy Initiative: Building nuclear power plants; Why do costs exceed projections?

46 *Financial Times*, 10 March 2016, Should investors be worried that EDF's finance director has resigned?

47 World Nuclear Association, Nuclear power in Russia, last updated December 2021.

48 Report of the UK's National Audit Office (NAO), *Hinkley Point C*, 23 June 2017.

49 The Paris Convention of 1960, and the Vienna Convention and the Brussels Convention, both of 1963.

50 Pope, A., *An Essay on Man*, 1734.

51 IEA, *Hydrogen Tracking Report.*

52 IEA, *Global Hydrogen Review*, 2021.

53 *KAPSARC*, December 2020, The Saudi move into hydrogen; A paradigm shift.

54 *Hydrogen Council*, 20 January 2020, Path to hydrogen competitiveness and cost perspective.

55 IEA, *Energy Technology Perspectives 2020: Special Report on Carbon Capture Use and Storage.*

56 *Ibid.*

57 *Guardian*, 16 May 2023, COP28 host UAE's approach is "dangerous" says UN ex-climate chief.

58 *Financial Times*, 17/18 December 2022, "Bottling the sun" is this a new dawn for fusion?

59 *Ibid.*

60 IEA, *Cooling Tracking Report*, November 2021.

61 IEA, *op. cit.*, September 2022.

62 *Global Cement*, 18 July 2022.

63 *CEMBUREAU*, 18 July 2022, European cement industry gears up for carbon neutrality by 2050.

64 *Bloomberg NEF*, 2 September 2019, How hydrogen could solve the steelmaking climate test and hobble coal.

65 World Steel Association, Blog: How hydrogen is gaining momentum in the Chinese steel industry, September 2020.

66 *Inside Climate News*, 9 December 2021, Inside climate energy: Batteries got cheaper in 2021. So how close are we to EVs that cost less than gasoline vehicles?

67 *EVvolumes.com*, Global EV sales for 2021.

68 Car Sales Statistics, 2021 (full year) Britain's new car market overview and analysis.

69 Energy in Demand, Weekly Review of Low Carbon Energy Transition, British Government Ditches plans for zero carbon houses, 11 July 2015.

70 *Bloomberg UK*, 30 November 2021, Electric vehicles may control half of major markets by 2030, Auto Execs predict.

71 *IRENA*, 2022, Critical materials for the energy transition: Lithium.

72 Especially neodymium, praseodymium, dysprosium, and terbium.

73 *Foreign Policy*, 21 May 2019, China raises threat of rare-earths cutoff to US.

74 Institute of Mechanical Engineers, Aviation industry agrees to reduce emissions, 7 October 2016.

75 IEA, *International Shipping Tracking Report*, September 2022.

76 *IMO Press Release*, 7 July 2023, IMO adopts revised strategy to reduce greenhouse gas emissions for international shipping.

Chapter 3

77 Kortenhulrst, J., CEO of RMI, a Colorado think tank, as reported by the FT on 14 November 2021.

78 IEA, *World Energy Investment*, 2021.

79 BlackRock web publication, 2022 climate-related shareholder proposals more prescriptive than 2021, 15 June 2023.

80 Task Force on Climate Related Financial Disclosure (TCFD), 2021 status report.

81 *Financial Times*, 19 March 2022, Boom in ESG ratings leaves a trail of confusion.

82 For instance the European Green Bond Standard, the Green Bond Principles, and the Climate Bonds Initiative.

83 Mike Zehetmayr, of Ernst and Young, quoted in the 19 March FT article.

84 Berg, F., *et al.*, *Aggregate Confusion: The Divergence of ESG Ratings.* MIT Sloan and the University of Zurich, version of 14 January 2022.

85 World Economic Forum, Deloitte, EY, KPMG, and PWC. Measuring stakeholder capitalism; Towards common metrics, consistent reporting, and sustainable value creation, September 2020.

86 *GreenPeace UK*, 23 March 2023, The Government isn't rising to the IPCC's challenge, but the climate movement will.

87 Friends of the Earth International, Climate justice and energy access, 6 April 2023.

88 Sierra Club, Climate and energy, *The Climate Crisis is Here*, 8 October 2018.

89 WWF Climate: Create a climate resilient and zero-carbon World, powered by renewable energy, 6 April 2023.

90 Friends of the Earth Press Release, 26 May 2021.

91 *BP Press Release*, 7 February 2023, bp integrated energy company strategy update.

92 *Financial Times*, 20 August 2022, Evidence of Lord Deben to the House of Commons Environmental Audit Committee.

93 Climate Change Committee, The numbers behind the budget: Six ways to explore the sixth carbon budget, 1 February 2021.

94 *Financial Times*, 22/23 July 2023, Tories urge Sunak to rein in green pledges after by-election carnage.

95 *Reuters*, 19 April 2023, German Cabinet approves bill to phase out oil and gas heating systems.

96 United Nations Development Programme (UNDP), People's climate vote, January 2021.

97 Li Jing, Does the Chinese public care about climate change? *China Dialogue*, September 2018.

Chapter 4

98 Mackenzie, W., Why the US oil industry could call for a carbon tax, *Opinion*, 29 April 2022.

99 *The Economist*, 19 September 2011, Do economists all favour a carbon tax?

100 World Resources Institute, Republican proposed "carbon dividend" is a great sign of progress. 10 February 2017.

101 Ocasio-Cortez, Democrats propose Green New Deal to counter climate change, *ABC News*, 7 February 2017.

102 Council on Foreign Relations, Envisioning a Green New Deal; a global comparison, updated February 2021.

103 *HM Government*, October 2021, Heat and buildings strategy.

104 *UK National Statistics*, 2022 provisional UK greenhouse gas emissions statistics, March 2023. Table 2 UK Territorial Carbon Dioxide Emissions by Sector.

105 IEA, *Key World Energy Statistics*.

106 *Statista*, 18 December 2022.

107 *Climate Home News*, 11 March 2022.

108 *China Daily*, 18 October 2017, Full text of Xi Jinping's report to the 19th CPC National Congress.

109 Center for Security and Emerging Technology: Translation of China's 14th Five Year Plan, May 2021.

110 *Politico Pro*, EU Reaches deal on critical climate policy after marathon.

111 AA, BMWi, BMU, BMZ, Steps towards an alliance for climate competitiveness and industry — Building blocks of a cooperative and open climate club. *BMF*, August 2021.

112 International Climate Finance, How the EU supports climate action in developing countries across the world. *European Commission*, 31 December 2022.

113 UK Climate Change Committee, 2022 progress report to Parliament; the CCC's annual assessment of UK progress in reducing emissions.

114 UK Department for Energy Security and Net Zero, 2022 UK greenhouse gas emissions, provisional figures, 30 March 2023.

115 *HM Government*, *op. cit.*

116 Committee on Climate Change, 2022 report to Parliament, *Progress in Reducing Emissions*, June 2022.

117 IEA, *India Energy Outlook*, 2021.

118 IEA, *Key World Energy Statistics*, 2021.

119 National statement of Prime Minister Shri Narendra Modi, *Indian Ministry of External Affairs*, 2 November 2021.

120 IEA, *India Energy Outlook*, 2021.

121 *Ibid.*

122 Carbon Tracker; South Africa, 28 October 2022.

123 Yelland, C., A look at South Africa's energy policies. *My Broadband*, 9 January 2021.

124 *IRENA*, October 2022, Indonesia Energy Transition Outlook.

125 IEA, *An Energy Sector Road Map to Net Zero Emissions in Indonesia*, September 2022.

126 OECD Development aid statistics.

127 *Reuters*, 15 November 2022, US, Japan and partners mobilise $20 billion to move Indonesia away from coal.

128 IEA, *Nigeria Energy Outlook*, 2019.

129 *Oxford Academic*, The Political Economy of Clean Energy Transitions, Chapter 20, E. Ogulaye, *Political Economy of Nigerian Power Sector Reform.*

130 *World Bank*, April 2023, Macro Poverty Outlook for Nigeria.

131 OECD Statistics.

132 *Oxford Academic, op. cit.*

133 *Financial Times*, 15 June 2023, Nigeria surprises with currency free float.

Chapter 5

134 Euractivity, Germany and France seek to match US green industry subsidies, 20 December 2022.

135 Our World Data: China CO_2 country profile.

136 *Emissions (data.gov.uk)*, 6 March 2022.

137 *Manorama Yearbook*, 17 November 2022, India and other BASIC nations oppose carbon border adjustment mechanisms.

138 *MIT Technical Review*, 15 February 2015, What happened to the rare earths crisis?

139 *Our World in Data*, 6 March 2022. Based on today's populations.

140 EU leaders split on giving nuclear power low-carbon status, 25/26 March 2023.

141 *Financial Times*, 10 February 2021, Prime Minister Narendra Modi's address to the World Sustainable Development Summit.

142 Evans, A., *et al.*, *UNA–UK Climate 2020: A Global Emissions Budget*. New York University, Centre on International Cooperation.

143 *OneIndia*, 22 October 2009, Indian emissions would never exceed those of developed nations.

144 *The Irrawaddy*, 25 September 2015, Indian Environment Minister: Less Poverty is.

145 *Narendra Modi web site*, 13 December 2015.

146 *Government of India*, India's intended nationally determined contribution, *Working Towards Climate Justice.*

147 IEA, *Africa Energy Outlook*, 2022.

148 *BBC*, 25 October 2022, COP27: Uganda-Tanzania oil pipeline sparks climate row.

149 *Euronews*, 19 October 2022, Uganda condemns EU resolution slamming oil pipeline.

150 UN Economic Commission for Africa, African Governance Report IV.

151 IEA, Financing clean energy transitions in emerging and developing economies, June 2021.

152 OECD Climate Finance Provided and Mobilised by Developed Countries; Aggregate Trends Updated with 2019 data, OECD, 2021.

153 *Gov.UK Press Release*, 16 May 2022, Foreign secretary launches new international development strategy.

154 Moreira da Silva, J., Leapfrogging to green: The world's energy transition depends on support to developing countries. *OECD*, 3 November 2021.

155 World Bank Group Annual Report 2021; Executive Summary.

156 World Bank Group Corporate Scorecards FY21 Update.

157 Chelsky, J., The challenge: How do we measure the mobilization of private capital? *World Bank Blog*, 2 August 2016.

158 Inter-America Investment Bank Annual Report 2021.

159 China is not included in the developed or the transitional countries listed at Annexes l and ll to the Treaty.

160 *Gov.UK*, 12 March 2015, UK announces plans to join the Asian Infrastructure Investment Bank.

161 *NATO Parliamentary Assembly*, 21 November 2020, China's belt and road initiative, a strategic and economic assessment.

162 *The Diplomat*, 25 June 2021.

163 Address of President Xi Jinping to the UN General Assembly, 21 September 2021.

164 *China's Overseas Development Finance*, 20 May 2022, Boston University Global Development Policy Center.

165 Mingey, M. and Kratz, A., *China's Belt and Road: Down But Not Out*, Rhodium Group Note, 4 January 2021.

166 NDRC.

167 International Institute for Sustainable Development, The Paris Agreement's new Article 6 rules, 13 December 2021.

168 *Environmental Defense Fund*, 4 December 2019, How carbon markets can increase climate ambition.

169 World Bank, *International Debt Report*, 2022.

170 *Ibid.*, 2021.

171 *Reuters*, 15 November 2022, US climate envoy wants development banks Overhall plan by April.

172 German Federal Ministry for Economic Co-operation, World Bank needs to restructure to address global challenges of the future, says Development Minister Schulze, 22 October 2022.

173 *The Hill*, 9 February 2021, Kerry says world cannot solve climate crisis without China.

174 *BBC News*, 4 November 2020, US formally withdraws from Paris Agreement.

175 *Reuters*, 4 November 2022, China says US must "take responsibility" for breakdown in climate ties.

176 *Financial Times*, 20 July 2023, US and China agree to revive climate talks ahead of UN summit.

Chapter 6

177 UNDP Director, UNDP energy hub, 14 July 2021.

178 The Agreement on an International Energy Programme.

179 The full membership of the IEA's Association is, Argentina, Brazil, China, Egypt, Indonesia, India, Morocco, Singapore, South Africa, and Thailand.

180 King James Bible, 1 Corinthians 14:8.

181 *The White House*, 22 June 2023, Joint Statement from the United States and India.

Appendix

182 Articles 57 and 63 of the UN Charter provide for the creation, with the approval of the General Assembly, of organisations under the UN umbrella which also has a degree of autonomy.

Postscript

183 Pope, A., An essay on criticism.

184 Umwelt Bundesamt (German Environment Ministry), Geoengineering, effective climate protection or Megalomania? April 2011.

185 Climate Engineering Governance Project of the Universities of Oxford, Sussex and UCL. Working Paper No. 1, May 2013.

Index

www.ingramcontent.com/pod-product-compliance
Lightning Source LLC
LaVergne TN
LVHW021055220926
848484LV00021B/907